WINNING
THE
INFLUENCE
GAME

WINNING THE INFLUENCE GAME

What Every Business Leader Should Know about Government

MICHAEL WATKINS, MICKEY EDWARDS, AND USHA THAKRAR

John Wiley & Sons, Inc.

New York • Chichester • Weinheim • Brisbane • Singapore • Toronto

Library of Congress Cataloging-in-Publication Data

Watkins, Michael, 1956–
  Winning the influence game : effective business strategies for managing government relations / Michael Watkins, Mickey Edwards, Usha Thakrar.
       p.   cm.
  Includes bibliographical references and index.
  ISBN 0-471-38361-9 (cloth : alk. paper)
  1. Industrial policy—United States.   2. Business and politics—United States.   I. Edwards, Mickey, 1937–   II. Thakrar, Usha, 1966–   III. Title.
  HD3616.U47 W34 2001
  658.4′012—dc21

                                                                2001017634

Printed in the United States of America.

10   9   8   7   6   5   4   3   2

To Shawna and Aidan.
M.W.

To Elizabeth.
M.E.

To John and Kavi.
U.T.

Contents

PART III

LOOKING FORWARD   191

Preface

American business operates in a political system designed to balance two fundamental but conflicting principles. The first of those fundamental principles is individual liberty. To a remarkable degree, American businesspeople are free to pursue their dreams without interference. This freedom has helped to create a nation of entrepreneurs, men and women who have devised countless new products and services to make our lives easier and more productive. Translated into economic terms, personal freedom is called *free enterprise*. It is the heart of the market system of economics, the engine of entrepreneurial achievement. This book is dedicated to the preservation of that important pillar of American life.

The other principle, just as strongly held and just as vital to America's economic strength, is the principle of self-government, the establishment of a system through which the American people collectively set rules to benefit the nation as a whole. The same Constitution that sets limits on government power and spells out the protection of individual rights also grants power to the federal government to regulate commerce and raise taxes and leaves immense power in the hands of state governments.

The same system that protects the entrepreneur's right to create and profit also grants to the public at large the power to set limits on the "free" aspect of free enterprise. This power—the authority to make the rules under which your business must operate—is a power exercised in many ways, and at many different levels of government. It resides in the courts, in hundreds of regulatory agencies, and in the Congress. And that covers only the federal level. By treaty, the United States has extended some of this power to international agencies located thousands of miles from

America's shores. And by spelling out clearly the powers of the federal government, the Constitution recognizes the authority of the states and local governments, each with their own systems of courts, regulatory agencies, and legislatures.

Simply put, it is a jungle out there, a thicket of competing and overlapping jurisdictions, regulators who at times pursue their own agendas, legislators whose expertise is limited but whose power is vast. It is the aim of this book to help you slash your way through that thicket and to avoid damaging rules and laws, and even to help shape rules and laws in ways that will enhance your ability to pursue your entrepreneurial dream.

Remember, it is your right to try to influence those laws and regulations. In a host of ways—from distributing governmental authority among separate power centers, to guaranteeing the right to petition the government for a redress of grievances—the Founding Fathers set out to make it exceedingly difficult for the government to do harm. The Supreme Court has affirmed that businesspeople (and all citizens) have a right to try to influence their government's actions in a variety of ways, including lobbying officeholders and contributing to political campaigns. The bottom line is this: It is your government, and you have a right, and sometimes an obligation, to help shape its decisions.

But that is easier said than done. How do you know where and when and how to intervene in the process? How does a company make its voice heard among all those seeking to influence government? This book will help you become an effective player in this all-important game of influencing governmental decision making.

Make no mistake: This book is not the final word on the subject of managing government relations. Such a book would run to thousands of pages and incorporate half a law library and hundreds of studies. Nor is this book intended to make your life easier. What we are proposing is real work: specific analyses and actions that will position your company to become a player in the shaping of laws and regulations that affect your success.

But keep this in mind: There will always be laws, regulations, and taxes. Government is not going to go away. Either you will influence those laws and regulations or your competition will. Either you will help devise the nature of the constraints and taxes under which you must operate—or the enhanced opportunities you will enjoy—or those decisions will be made by politicians and public policy advocates pursuing their own very different agendas. What follows is a specific game plan designed to make you a player, not a victim.

This is not a book to be read and set aside. Use the worksheets we provide to think through your goals, your assets, the obstacles governments may pose, potential coalition partners, and potential adversaries. Make a commitment to get to know the men and women who represent you in government, and to learn which agency officials and which legislators are the key decision makers on the issues that affect your company. This is a how-to book. But knowing how to do something is only half the battle. We will give you the tools to become an effective participant in the decisions that will affect your company's future. The rest is up to you.

How This Book Was Started

This book originated in conversations between two of the authors in 1995 when we were colleagues at the Kennedy School of Government. We found that we shared an interest in how businesses influence government, Michael Watkins because of his studies of coalition building and international trade negotiations and Mickey Edwards because of his experience in Congress and extensive writing on our system of government. We agreed that most corporate executives are unprepared to deal with government and uncertain how to protect themselves against harmful government intervention—fewer yet know how to actively shape rule-making processes in advantageous ways. We also observed that most MBA programs do little to prepare aspiring business leaders in this domain, leaving them to learn by doing (often by making unnecessary mistakes).

When we went looking for books written explicitly for business leaders describing how to play the influence game, we did not find any. We were initially surprised, but eventually came up with at least four explanations for this state of affairs. First, the impact of government has never been integrated into the frameworks that most businesses use to develop their strategies. Second, government is often viewed solely as an impediment and rarely as a potential resource. Third, many business leaders react with a reflexive distaste to the idea of involving themselves in politics. Finally, few business academics are deeply familiar with—or, for that matter, interested in—the messy workings of government. Together these factors have conspired to keep government relations something of a backwater, a corporate staff function that reports to the legal department and not a central player in the formulation and implementation of business strategy. We resolved to write a book that would highlight the strategic role of government relations and provide guidance for business leaders on how to play the influence game. We sketched out an outline, but we were both immersed in other projects at the time and left it at that.

Our conversations resumed in 1998 after Michael moved to the Harvard Business School and began his work on corporate diplomacy. This time our discussions also involved Usha Thakrar. She suggested that we conduct an exploratory survey of government relations professionals in Fortune 100 companies, to find out how their companies organize to influence. The results suggested a very wide divergence in the importance that businesses attached to influencing government and in the ways they organized to influence. The survey also confirmed our early suspicion that most senior managers are woefully ignorant about the workings of government. We then conducted an extensive series of interviews with people involved in the influence game and formulated the model presented in this book.

In developing our ideas, we consulted politicians and regulators as well as corporate government relations professionals and independent lobbyists who have had striking success in influencing the workings of government.

Acknowledgments

Our heartfelt thanks go to the following people for sharing their wisdom with us: Wright Andrews, Tommy Boggs, Dick Cheney,

Don Clay, Neil Cohen, Tom Downey, Ken Duberstein, Peter Frank, Ann Gosier, David Greenberg, Andy Grenier, Noreen Holthaus, Todd Hullin, Mike Johnson, Tom Korologos, Mike Kostiw, Bill Lane, Jim LeBlanc, Tom Mohr, Heather Mullen, Larry Nichols, Paul O'Neill, Dennis Thomas, Sue Tierney, Candace Vessella, Anne Wexler, and Lyn Withey. Our thanks also to those who provided valuable insights but asked not be named. We interviewed many business leaders and government relations professionals and have drawn numerous illustrative quotes and stories directly from those interviews. As a condition of the interviews, however, we agreed not to identify the sources of quotes. We believe that this approach permitted the people we interviewed to share their experiences with candor.

Three people deserve special mention for their work in support of this project. The first is Ann Goodsell, who provided invaluable editorial guidance in helping us think about the structure of the book and communicate our ideas with clarity. The second is Terri Zavada, a highly skilled and experienced government relations professional who assisted us with the research for this book and offered many suggestions that substantially improved the manuscript. The third is our agent, Barbara Rifkind, who worked tirelessly on our behalf.

At the Harvard Business School, Dean Kim Clark, David Garvin, Earl Sasser, Jim Sebenius, and Mike Wheeler have been a constant support to Michael. The work of Pankaj Ghemawat, Barry Nalbuff, Adam Brandenburger, and Michael Porter was instrumental in shaping his understanding of "the games businesses play." Working with Charan Devereaux on cases involving the impact of business on international trade policy deepened his understanding of the global-influence game and contributed a number of powerful illustrations of our concepts.

Throughout the writing of this book, Mickey talked frequently with the men and women he had worked with in Congress, among them effective lobbyists, members of the Congressional staff, and veterans of the White House and other government agencies. They contributed substantially to his understanding of effective government relations organization and strategy.

During the early stages of researching and writing, John Farr and Prem Das provided valuable insights and support to Usha. Their unique perspectives on how this book could be most helpful to a business executive helped shape the final structure.

The research for this book was supported by the Division of Research at the Harvard Business School. We very much appreciate the encouragement given to this project by Research Directors Teresa Amabile and Mike Yoshino.

MICHAEL WATKINS
MICKEY EDWARDS
USHA THAKRAR

Cambridge, Massachusetts
November 2000

Introduction:
The Influence Game

I believe that over the next few years, the future of the
Internet will be determined more by policy choices
than technology choices.

Steve Case, CEO, America Online
New York Times, July 13, 1999

Managers who ignore the actions of government do so at great
risk. Government rule makers—legislative and regulatory, local,
state, and federal, domestic and foreign—play critical roles in
shaping the playing fields on which businesses compete. Governments make and enforce rules that impinge on every dimension of
company strategy and operations. How are the rules of the competitive game made and enforced? Largely through a competition
for influence on governmental rule makers and referees.[1]

Make no mistake about it: The rule-making game is every bit
as competitive as selling products and services. It just takes place
in a different arena and with a different set of players—corporations and governments, but also unions, consumer, and environmental organizations, and other interest groups. As one
government relations professional put it, "Decisions made by government impact everything we do. . . . You have to have the pa-
tience to understand how to shape them over a long period
of time."

Both to gain a competitive advantage and to avoid harm, therefore, businesses must know how to influence government. This is a matter of more than just developing good strategies. It also means having the organizational capacity to execute and follow through. Because if *you* do not organize to influence the rules of the game, *others* surely will.

Rule Making in the New Economy

Government has had an impact on business for as long as both institutions have existed. Even so, the ability to influence governmental rule making has probably never been more critically important, to companies large and small, than it is today. There are at least three reasons why businesses need to be more active in influencing government:

1. Government involvement in business is growing. From increased antitrust scrutiny to greater involvement by the courts in settling business conflicts, government is playing an increasing role in decisions that affect business. "The impact of government on business is going up," one government relations professional observes. "The influence of the party in power only adjusts the slope of the line. The line still goes up."

2. Technological innovations are changing the way the world works, in every sphere from communications to manufacturing processes to how we run our homes and, in some cases, even how we conceive our children. These advances are creating new challenges for both business and government. Already we are witnessing the beginnings of rule making efforts to grapple with what the *New York Times* called "a convergence of technology that has far outpaced laws, court opinions, and regulatory decisions."[2]

3. We are in the midst of a fundamental restructuring of the economy, driven by new technology that is impacting all sectors of business. In *Information Rules*, Carl Shapiro and Hal Varian assert that "No executive in the technology sector can

ignore the government's role in the information economy."[3] And neither can anyone else.

The rules of the new economy have yet to be written. Those who do not participate in the crafting of those rules risk being left behind. From now on, policy making will shape the evolution of every sector of our economy and will impact business strategy in a wide array of ways. The advent of the Internet and other technological advances is changing the way all business is done. How the rules that govern these new arenas get written will even affect those who do business in more traditional arenas. Consider these examples:

- *Government determines who owns what information.* From stock quotes to book sales data to personal credit information, computer technology and the Internet are making vast amounts of personal information readily available to anyone with a computer. Federal and state governments are struggling to establish the rules that govern ownership and access to many types of information. A 1999 court battle between the *New York Times* and the online bookseller Amazon.com over who owned the *New York Times* Bestseller List is just one example.[4] Another is a recent Federal Trade Commission (FTC) action against Toysmart, a bankrupt online toy company that had collected information from over 200,000 people, many of them children, sometimes allegedly in violation of the Children's Online Privacy Protection Act of 1998. Creditors seeking to recover their money were pressing the company to sell its databases and customer files. This situation raised alarms among regulators and privacy advocates. In addition to the FTC's action, 38 states filed briefs objecting to the sale, and Senators Patrick Leahy (D-VT) and Robert Torricelli (D-NJ) introduced legislation to bar the sale. In a July 2000 settlement with the FTC, the company agreed to destroy information it had collected on children after the Children's Privacy Act came into force. Toysmart was permitted to sell the remaining information, but only to a "qualified buyer"—a business in the family-oriented market that would agree to restrictions on how the data would be used.[5]

- *Government influences which standards dominate and how they are developed.* As *Business Week* reported in 1999, "All it took was a good, hard push from the Federal Communications Commission. And suddenly television manufacturers and the cable service industry, so long at odds over the technical standards for delivering digital programming, have shaken hands on a plan."[6] The agreement deals with technical specifications for the connection that will bring digital imaging to a television set through existing cable systems. The two groups had been wrangling for years when the FCC warned that it would set standards for them if they could not do so themselves.

  Qualcomm's success in winning acceptance for its CDMA wireless technology in China is another example. The company had the support of the U.S. government, which had linked the deal to approval of Chinese entry into the World Trade Organization (WTO). The Chinese Ministry of Information Industry had effectively ordered the country's second ranking phone company, Unicom, to adopt CDMA. All that remained, it appeared, was for Qualcomm to negotiate a framework agreement with the Ministry. But the Chinese were actually leaning toward a rival European technology while trying not to antagonize the United States. The negotiations almost failed and Unicom almost went with the rival technology until Qualcomm CEO, Irwin Jacobs, with the help of former National Security Adviser Brent Scowcroft negotiated a last minute deal.[7]

- *Government places restrictions on mergers, alliances, and acquisitions.* The new economy has spawned a wave of megamergers—MCI and WorldCom, AOL and Time Warner, AT&T and Media One, to name a few. Regulators seldom block mergers outright (though it occasionally happens, as in the case of Sprint and WorldCom), but they do impose significant restrictions on the resulting companies' post-merger structure. In late 1999, for example, the FTC approved the merger of Exxon and Mobil, creating the world's largest oil company. The conditions? The new company was required to divest 2,431 gasoline stations, pipeline interests, and a refinery. Mergers are also being scrutinized harder internationally. European antitrust regulators were instrumental, for example, in killing the Sprint-WorldCom deal and are likely to reshape others, such as the AOL-Time Warner merger.

- *Government decides what can and cannot be exported.* From satellites and supercomputers to seemingly ordinary technologies like medical devices, government controls on exports can affect an astonishing array of products. Two recent controversies illustrate what is at stake. Developers of encryption software worried that national security restrictions on the export of encryption tools would give foreign manufacturers a competitive advantage. After several years of lobbying to refute claims of risk to national security, encryption companies convinced the Clinton administration to relax the restrictions. Satellite companies are now facing a different challenge. In the wake of accusations that satellite companies gave sensitive information on rocket guidance to the Chinese, Congress transferred the permitting process for satellite exports from the Commerce Department to the much stricter State Department.

- *Government imposes taxes.* When you buy something on the Internet, do you pay sales tax? If so, do you pay it to the state where you live or to the state where the seller is located? These are among the tricky questions facing Congress today. At the center of the debate are the states, which want to tax all Internet sales; traditional stores, which lose sales to the Internet because online purchases are tax free; online stores, which do not want to charge sales tax; and the federal government, which is trying to sort it all out. The resulting decisions could permanently alter the nature of retail business.

Congress is also weighing efforts to clamp down on tax shelters. In mid-2000, for example, PriceWaterhouseCoopers (PwC) came under embarrassing scrutiny in Congress over its Bond and Option Sales Strategy (BOSS), a plan designed to use offshore transactions to create large paper tax losses. PwC reportedly had to return money to clients and some tax experts involved with it left the firm.[8]

Global Rule Making

Advancing globalization has set the stage for a new wave of negotiated global rule making involving national governments and supranational agencies in such arenas as trade, investment, and antitrust. As the following examples illustrate, the ability to influence international rule makers is a core strategic skill for U.S. companies doing business abroad:

- Between 1992 and 1998, cases with an international dimension grew from less than 5 percent to more than 30 percent of the caseload of the U.S. Justice Department Antitrust Division.[9] This shift is raising new questions about which governments and agencies have jurisdiction over competition policy. Before approving the Boeing-McDonnell Douglas merger, for example, the European Union successfully pressed for European carriers' participation in contracts previously assigned exclusively to U.S. airlines.

- As the European Union moved to establish uniform standards for product testing, the U.S. Commerce Department became alarmed that the result could be a commercial version of "fortress Europe." But efforts to negotiate a U.S.-European Union (EU) agreement on testing processes in seven sectors—pharmaceuticals, medical devices, telecom, electrical safety, electromagnetic compatibility, pleasure boats, and veterinary biologics—went nowhere until a newly formed international business coalition, the Transatlantic Business Dialogue, helped drive the process to a successful conclusion in 1997.

- A new supranational body, the World Trade Organization (WTO), was established by the 1993 Uruguay Round of the GATT to oversee the world trading system and to adjudicate disputes. WTO rulings are having a growing impact on the rules for international business. In 1999, the United States won the first round in a trade battle when the EU accepted a WTO finding in the so-called "banana war" and agreed to rework its import rules. This outcome followed a vigorous lobbying campaign by Chiquita Brands and CEO Carl Lindner. In the second round, Washington is fighting a 10-year EU ban on U.S. beef containing certain growth hormones. In 1999, the WTO ruled that the United States is entitled to impose almost $117 million in duties to make up for the trade loss.[10] The American beef industry claims that the ban has cost producers $250 million a year and has lobbied hard to get Congress to approve sanctions against European producers.[11]

- In 1994 Enron, a Houston-based energy company, was awarded a contract to build a $2.9 billion power plant in Dabhol, India. The project was an outgrowth of the economic policies of then-Prime Minister Narasimha Rao. But when a rival political party took over India's national and state governments in mid-1995, state officials canceled the Dabhol project, citing padded costs and high electricity rates.[12] After months of bitter negotiations, Enron renegotiated the contract but had to accept an 11 percent cut in the overall price tag, lower electricity rates, and a partnership with the state-owned utility.[13]

The bottom line is this: To develop and pursue strategies for growth amid the turbulence caused by advancing globalization, U.S. companies must be adept at understanding and shaping governmental rule-making processes anywhere they do business.

Local Rule Making

As the influence game becomes more global, it is simultaneously becoming more local. Tools and techniques employed to influence government at the federal level and internationally are increasingly being employed to influence state and local politics. Companies that ignore rule making at these levels, or who underestimate the sophistication of their opponents, can end up being blindsided.

Disney's high-profile failure to build a theme park near Haymarket, Virginia, illustrates some classic pitfalls for companies dealing with local politics. In 1993, Disney announced that it had purchased 3,000 acres of farmland 25 miles from Washington and would build "Disney's America," a $650-million historical theme park, golf courses, over 2,000 residential units, and 2 million square feet of retail and office space.[14] To get the land at a reasonable cost, Disney had proceeded in secret.[15]

The company had won the governor's firm support and had wrested $163 million in incentives from the Virginia legislature to support road building, worker training, and promotion of tourism. Prince William County officials, who expected the park and related development near Haymarket to create 3,000 new jobs and generate $12 million a year in county tax revenue, were also wholeheartedly on board and prepared to issue the necessary permits.

A year after its initial announcement, Disney announced that it would seek an alternative site for the park; ultimately the company abandoned the project altogether. The company had failed to build public support and suffered a barrage of criticism, including a raft of editorials and other opinion pieces. Critics singled out a planned "Industrial Revolution" attraction that would speed riders through mock molten metal and past ironclad ships fighting near a Civil War fort. Others criticized the company's initial plans for not addressing the issue of slavery.

The core opposition consisted of a coalition of local landowners concerned about the impact of traffic, historians who saw the park as a vulgarization of U.S. history, and national environmental groups such as the Sierra Club and the Natural Resources Defense Council. Over 60 groups eventually opposed the project, including one called Protect Historic America representing artists and intellectuals such as novelist William Styron and historian Shelby Foote.

Disney tried to recover, launching a public relations campaign in support of the project and hiring historians as consultants. Disney's Chairman, Michael Eisner, bluntly stated, "If the people think we will back off, they are mistaken." Eisner also expressed his belief that the park would foster an interest in history among young people. "I was dragged to Washington as a kid," he was quoted as saying, "and it was the worst weekend of my life. I promise you 90 percent of the kids in America don't know who lived in Mount Vernon, Montpelier, or Monticello." Eisner received a stinging rebuke from historian C. Vann Woodward, a Pulitzer Prize winner: "This strikes me as the view of a very ordinary type of mind that one encounters among the illiterate." Another historian remarked that "Disney's specialty is to sentimentalize everything that it touches."

Disney modified the park's design to try to address some of these concerns but critics pounced again when the press reported that the park would let visitors "experience" slavery.[16] The Black History Action Coalition threatened a boycott if the topics of the Civil War and slavery were not excluded altogether.[17] Eisner responded by calling such an action "censorship," declaring that "We're not going to put people in chains." Even Congress got involved when the Senate held hearings on the proposed development.

Disney ultimately decided to throw in the towel when several lawsuits threatened to further delay the project. "It was the uncertainty of the timing," one official was quoted as saying. Peter Rummell, the president of Disney Design and Development, concurred: "Despite our confidence that we would eventually win the necessary approvals," he explained, "it has become clear that we could not say when the park would be open—or even when we could break ground."[18]

Disney made a classic mistake: It tried to do a quiet deal with those it thought were the key decision makers, only to see the deal fall apart. It neglected, until too late, the role of public opinion. The company also underestimated the ability of the opposition to use other branches and levels of government, such as the judiciary and the Senate. In this situation, as in many cases involving government, delay was as good as defeat.

The main take-away message is that you have to be able to play the influence game wherever you do business. Every time you want to pursue a major project, you have to consider, and be prepared to influence, local politics. The good news is that the model presented in this book can be applied to influence games at any level of government, local, state, national, or international.

A Dangerous State of Ignorance

Given the importance of rule making, it is astonishing how many otherwise savvy business executives appear not to understand how government works and what it can do to their companies. In our survey of government relations professionals at Fortune 100 companies, 77 percent rated the typical senior executive as having a mediocre—or worse—grasp of the way governmental processes work.[19] This is a dangerous level of ignorance. As the foregoing examples suggest, governments at all levels will continue to have a significant impact on business. Not understanding what that impact is likely to be, or how to influence it, constitutes the loss of a potential strategic opportunity.

Many leaders see government as nothing more than a nuisance. According to one CEO:

> There are an unfortunate number of CEOs of surprisingly large companies that don't want to deal with Washington. They are either afraid or don't understand or really think it is an unreasonable imposition on their time. They feel that they ought to be able to run their business and that Washington shouldn't always be bothering them. And, therefore, there is an "I'm going to ignore them and maybe if I ignore them they'll go away" type attitude.

While one can understand the emotion behind it, that's not the way the world works. This attitude is commonplace in many growing high-tech companies. When Bill Gates opened Microsoft's tiny

Washington office in 1995, he told his employees, "I'm sorry that we have to have a Washington presence. We thrived during our first 16 years without any of this."[20] Gates' attitude is typical of many executives in entrepreneurial information-age companies. An attorney who has represented Silicon Valley companies in antitrust dealings with the federal government pointed out the risks of this stance:

> The perspective of a lot of companies I worked with is that Washington is irrelevant to high technology. "What do they have to do with anything? What do these clumsy agency infrastructures have to do with anything?" Then they make an acquisition and find out that what is and isn't a monopoly is defined by government.

Ironically, the businesses that are creating emerging industries and driving the new wave of globalization are the most likely to be impacted by government legislation and regulation and the least prepared to help shape the rules. Successful companies in established industries—Merck, General Motors, General Electric, Boeing, and the like—learned to play the rule making game a long time ago. They established Washington offices, developed relationships with regulators and legislators, joined industry associations, built coalitions, and made working with government a core strategic goal. A government relations professional at a Fortune 100 company comments, "You need to have a deliberate strategy to integrate government relations into day-to-day activities. Government relations must have a place at the senior management table." These companies may not always win, but they know how to put up a good fight. The companies that until recently operated out of garages and now stand poised to dominate industries are discovering that they have to learn to play the rule making game, too.

Playing the Game to Win

Developing a strategy and influencing the rule makers and referees in government is much easier with a road map. The rest of this book provides exactly that. Drawing on case studies and interviews with top executives, government relations professionals, legislative and regulatory staff, and professional lobbyists, as well as our own hands-on experience, we provide practical insight into developing successful strategies for influencing government. From diagnosing government's impact on your business to organizing to influence to building coalitions, we will provide specific guidelines for businesses of all sizes.

While many of the examples that we use are drawn from efforts to influence rule makers in Washington, our model is a very general one. The basic principles outlined in Chapter 1 can be applied just as effectively in developing campaigns to influence state and local government as they can at the federal and international levels.

CHAPTER 1

Fundamental Principles

What do you need to understand about how the influence game is played? We have distilled seven fundamental principles for influencing rule making from our interviews with professional Washington lobbyists, corporate government relations professionals, and government officials. These principles provide the basis for a practical, results-oriented approach to influence that we will develop throughout the course of this book.

Principle 1: Never Discount the Potential Impact of Government

Whenever government intervenes, the stakes are high for all concerned. As Jim Barksdale, the former CEO of Netscape Communications, once commented, "We've observed first-hand how government can help or hinder the technology industry. We've learned that working with the government is far more productive than trying to ignore it."[1] Some companies understand this better than others.

Government actions can impose huge costs on businesses. This is widely acknowledged when the interests of businesses clash with those of nonbusiness organizations, such as environmental and consumer groups. But governments often play central roles in shaping the course of cooperation and competition *among* businesses as well.

The failed merger of WorldCom and Sprint is a case in point. In late 1999 Sprint, America's third-largest long-distance carrier, agreed to merge with WorldCom in a $115 billion deal that would have solidified WorldCom's position as the leading challenger to AT&T in global telecommunications. A merger with Sprint was to be the capstone of WorldCom's growth-through-M&A strategy—a strategy that had turned WorldCom from a small Mississippi-based reseller of AT&T long-distance service into a global telecommunications powerhouse with 77,000 employees in 65 countries and 1999 revenues exceeding $37 billion. Eight months later, the WorldCom/Sprint deal was dead, killed not by shareholders or Wall Street analysts, but by European and U.S. antitrust regulators.

Although WorldCom had undertaken more than 70 acquisitions in a decade, including that of the much larger MCI Corporation, the company continued to view itself as part of the solution to the anticompetitive practices of the past, not as part of the problem.[2] From the moment the Sprint deal was announced, according to the *Washington Post*, WorldCom CEO Bernard Ebbers "branded as ignorant anyone who suggested it might not gain approval." The *Post* further noted that "those close to WorldCom say [Ebbers] simply could not conceive of his company—so long a scrappy underdog in the battle with AT&T—as a force that could be seen as a threat to competition."[3]

Warning signs that the deal was in trouble surfaced early. On the day the merger was announced, the chairman of the Federal Communications Commission stated that the companies "will bear a heavy burden to show how consumers would be better off."[4] Regulators in Washington state soon expressed reservations about the impact on consumers and signaled their intent to challenge the combination.[5] The deal subsequently ran into trouble with

European Union antitrust officials, ostensibly over the unhealthy concentration it would create in Internet services. *The Economist* speculated that WorldCom's problems with the EU stemmed in part from "the shabby way WorldCom behaved in acquiring MCI. It first promised to spin off some MCI holdings to Cable & Wireless to satisfy regulatory concerns, and then did so in such a halfhearted way (it stole back employees and kept customers) that the British firm had to take it to court (C&W settled for $200 million)." As a result, WorldCom was viewed within the EU as "an untrustworthy predator."[6] In the United States, regulators had reportedly told CEO Ebbers, "Don't come back soon with another big one like this."[7]

In June 2000, after negotiations between the company and antitrust regulators failed to reach fruition, Attorney General Janet Reno announced that the Justice Department would sue to block the deal. This was the largest merger that had ever been challenged by the Justice Department. One day later, European antitrust authorities announced that they too had formally rejected the deal. Government opposition surprised many Wall Street analysts, and led the *Wall Street Journal* to question whether there was "a widening disconnect between Wall Street, where the deals get done, and government power centers such as Washington and Brussels, where they must pass regulatory muster." One analyst was quoted as commenting, "There's a certain aspect of Washington that Wall Street doesn't get." Another noted that credible early insider reports that the Justice Department would oppose the deal had been discounted.[8] The failed deal called into question the viability of WorldCom's basic strategy for growth and led observers to speculate that the company would itself become an acquisition target.

The stakes are just as high, if not higher, for businesses far smaller than WorldCom. Ignoring the potential impacts of new regulations can significantly affect your bottom line. For example, a $60 million wholesaler of heating, ventilation, and air-conditioning equipment watched its 1999 profits get eaten up by a lawsuit for violating a minor clause of the Americans with

Disabilities Act (ADA). The company's executives failed to pay close enough attention to how the ADA impacted their business, and the resulting settlement turned a 25 percent increase in profits into a 3 percent loss.

Not all government intervention has a negative impact on business, of course. Some businesses and industries are able to play the rule making game to their advantage. A coalition of established gambling casino companies, for example, took a potentially damaging situation and turned it to their own ends. In 1996, Congress established a commission to rein in gambling, which observers viewed as a first step toward imposing restrictions like those on tobacco and alcohol. In 1999, the commission called for measures ranging from a ban on Internet gambling to a ban on the sale of lottery tickets to minors. However, the bulk of the recommendations targeted the new entrants in the business that had been eroding the market share of "big gambling." By forming a trade association led by some top-tier Washington lobbyists, big gambling had influenced the composition of the commission, made some early painless concessions, and channeled the focus toward its direct competitors—the Internet, state lotteries, and Native American casinos. The net result was a set of recommendations that left big gambling with a more secure position in the marketplace.[9]

The bottom line is that in spheres ranging from privacy issues to labor laws to industry deregulation, government can affect any company's well-being. Working with government will not always achieve the desired results, but it is better to anticipate and work to shape the impact of government actions than to struggle to respond to them after the fact. You have to organize to influence.

Principle 2: Effective Influence Is Built on a Foundation of Relationships

You have to build a foundation of relationships with rule makers and potentially influential allies *before* you need them. "Too often companies wait until it is too late, just before or after a regulation has been passed," observes one government relations professional. "You can't expect to have an impact at that point." You have to build relationships to exert influence. The capacity to do so depends in turn on senior executives' willingness to work with government, to cultivate potential allies, and to allocate the necessary resources—including their own time. As one professional lobbyist points out:

> CEOs . . . will talk about themselves as victims of government. They never think of themselves as partners. The trick is to always understand that you will have a seat at the table. People will be glad to see you and glad to talk to you and glad to understand the impact on your business of the decisions they're making.

Some companies understand the value of organizing to influence and some do not. Compare, for example, the recent antitrust cases against Microsoft and Intel. Microsoft's response was to attack the Justice Department with both barrels in a last minute public battle. By contrast, Intel took advantage of years of experience and a wealth of relationships to minimize the damage.

The Justice Department initially sought a court order to stop Microsoft from forcing PC manufacturers to install Internet Explorer with the Windows operating system, arguing that this use of Microsoft's dominant market position was predatory behavior designed to drive its competitor Netscape out of business. Microsoft called the charges ludicrous and began negotiating with the Justice Department, but to little effect. Finally, Attorney General Janet Reno declared that Microsoft had "restricted the choices available for consumers in America and the world,"[10] and the Justice Department filed suit in federal court in 1998.[11] Microsoft then employed a variety of tactics to delay the trial. They also used public relations practices that backfired, generating negative press that significantly damaged the company's public image.

Virtually simultaneously, the Federal Trade Commission (FTC) sued Intel, asserting that as a weapon in patent disputes it had withheld technical data from companies that were customers for its microprocessors but potential competitors in other areas of business. Intel negotiated and settled the suit in 1999. Intel's handling of the process facilitated the settlement: Intel began direct negotiations with the FTC before the suit was filed and continued until the suit was settled. The company assigned a single spokesperson to handle all inquiries and said as little as possible in public about the FTC, the process, or the merits of the suit. Compared to the Microsoft antitrust case, the Intel suit went virtually unnoticed.

Microsoft, because of its apparent disdain of government and consequent failure to build a foundation to work with government, has had to play catch-up. The company has made some costly mistakes on its way up the learning curve. Intel executives, by contrast, had established a presence in Washington with a track record of effective dealings. Intel had lobbied to influence trade with Japan early on. The company had also cooperated with the FTC in prior antitrust inquiries and had gained a reputation in Washington as a thoughtful and forthright source of analysis on proposed combinations in the industry. The two companies' different approaches to dealing with government had predictable impacts on the results of their respective cases.

You need to anticipate what relationships with rule makers—and those who influence them—will be crucial to helping you influence government. Then you have to invest in developing those relationships so you have some capital to draw on when you need it.

Principle 3: To Shape the Rules, You Have to Build Coalitions

Whatever the objective, individual companies are seldom equipped to influence rule making on their own. This is especially true of small to medium-sized businesses that lack the resources and reach of Fortune 100 companies. As one government relations professional put it, "If you're smaller, you have to figure out how to build a coalition quickly. The key to that is partnering, not only with your potential customer but perhaps with others who are in the same league—same size, whatever—because there are very few things that any one individual can do." This is why marketplace competitors form industry associations and other alliances. According to our survey of government relations professionals at Fortune 100 companies, those companies belong to an average of 28 trade associations; some belong to as many as 300, excluding informal groups and short-lived coalitions organized around time-limited initiatives.

The members of a coalition may be long-standing allies who cooperate on a broad range of issues, such as industry associations. Take, for example, USA Engage, a coalition of over 600 corporations and associations—including Caterpillar, Boeing, DuPont, General Motors, IBM, Motorola, USX, the U.S. Chamber of Commerce, the American Petroleum Institute, the Business Roundtable, and the Environmental Export Council—that promotes international economic involvement by U.S. business and discourages unilateral economic sanctions by the U.S. government for political purposes. Other coalitions are formed for specific ad hoc purposes. One example is the coalition of businesses and organizations that formed to oppose the Family and Medical Leave Act of 1993, including the U.S. Chamber of Commerce, the Small Business Association, the National Retail Federation, and 42 other groups. The coalition was unsuccessful in defeating the legislation, but significantly influenced its ultimate content.

Sometimes the participants in a coalition are strange bedfellows—a mix of business and nonbusiness organizations. For example, the coalition that supported the merger of railroad giants CSX and Norfolk Southern included environmental groups who favored a reduction in the number of transport trucks on the road. Though likely to disagree on most other issues, they were able to create a potent alliance to achieve a specific, narrow set of complementary objectives.

To build coalitions, you have to identify groups with complementary goals, build alliances among them, and focus their collective resources to shape a particular rule making process. At its core, in other words, effective coalition building is about identifying and exploiting alignments of interests. You need to identify your interests and goals and then ask questions like "Who shares these interests? Can we agree on a common approach?" Look within the industry and then across industries. You also have to know how to build momentum, such as by approaching potential allies in the right order at the right time so you maximize the likelihood that you will get them on board.

Principle 4: To Influence the Rules, You Need to Cooperate with Your Competitors

Effective efforts to influence government involve a mix of cooperation and competition with other influential players. This mirrors what goes on in the marketplace: in *Co-opetition*, Barry Nalebuff and Adam Brandenburger describe business strategy as a game involving four sets of players, three of whom—competitors, customers, suppliers—are familiar.[12] But they add a crucial fourth category, *complementors*—companies whose goods and services complement each other. Microsoft and Intel, the two halves of the so-called Wintel duopoly, are classic complementors: Better hardware helps Microsoft sell more software, and first-rate programs help Intel sell more microprocessors.

In the marketplace, competitors compete and complementors complement. In the rule making game, however, competitors often cooperate and complementors sometimes compete. In what the *Wall Street Journal* characterized as an illustration of how "rivals used to tussling can unite when faced with a threat to their trading franchises," three of the largest and most competitive securities firms joined forces to lobby the Securities and Exchange Commission (SEC) to overhaul the system for trading in the U.S. stock market.[13] The companies—Goldman Sachs, Merrill Lynch, and Morgan Stanley Dean Witter—urged the SEC to lower some of the New York Stock Exchange's barriers to competition and to facilitate trading on the new electronic exchanges.

The reverse can also be true: Companies that cooperate in the marketplace can end up competing to shape rule making and refereeing processes. Auto manufacturers and their dealers enjoy a classic symbiotic relationship. Recently, however, General

Motors has been in conflict with its dealers over the future of automobile retailing, whose competitive nature is being changed by the Internet. In Texas, for example, General Motors created an Internet showroom to enable customers to purchase used vehicles online. Under pressure from dealers, the state denied GM a license to do business as a retailer and prevented launch of the Web site.[14]

Likewise, Ford and Bridgestone/Firestone had a long-standing business relationship that came under severe strain because of intervention by legislators and regulators. In early May of 2000, the National Highway Traffic Safety Administration (NHTSA) launched an investigation of fatal accidents linked to tire separation problems on Ford's Explorer SUVs. This investigation spurred Bridgestone/Firestone to recall 6.5 million tires in early August. Subsequent questions about whether the companies should have reported problems earlier led to civil lawsuits, a federal criminal investigation, and high-profile hearings in Congress.[15] Statements made during and after the hearings suggested that the companies were seeking to pin the blame on each other—essentially jockeying to influence the referees.

Competitors' efforts to cooperate to influence government create tension in top executives' dealings with each other. But the savviest are able to manage this tension, competing vigorously for market share but knowing when and how to cooperate in the rule-making game.

To be effective in influencing government, you therefore have to be open to cooperating with your competitors to advance shared interests. This can be tough to do, especially if intense competition has resulted in personal animosities. But it is often worth the effort to break down these barriers, even if you have to create whole new organizations to coordinate your influence activities.

Principle 5: Where You Play Is as Important as How You Play

Government in the United States is highly complex. Typically, there are multiple forums at which rule making activity can take place. Within the executive branch alone, antitrust issues can be handled by the Justice Department or the Federal Trade Commission; other agencies such as the Federal Communications Commission and the Federal Aviation Administration review deals in their respective industries. Likewise, environmental regulations can be written by the Environmental Protection Agency, the Department of Interior, or the Department of Energy. While Congress is considering a piece of legislation, a regulatory agency may be deciding whether to file a lawsuit on the same issue. Finally, the same issue may be on the agendas of state, federal, and foreign governments, with the result that outcomes at different levels interact unpredictably.

The tobacco industry has been facing civil actions brought by individuals and lawsuits brought by state governments for a number of years. After losing ground in these forums, the industry is now facing an unprecedented lawsuit at the federal level. In 1999, the Justice Department filed suit against major cigarette manufacturers, accusing them of conspiring "to defraud and mislead the public about the health effects of smoking."[16] The tobacco industry is also facing possible challenges at the global level. The U.N. World Health Organization has begun exploratory talks on an international treaty to curb tobacco use and advertising.[17]

Managing conflicting rules imposed by different levels of government can be difficult. In Massachusetts, for example, commercial developers must contend with two sets of rules governing access to people with disabilities, the guidelines of the state Architectural Access Board (AAB) and the federal Americans with Disabilities Act (ADA). The AAB rules apply in some cases, the ADA rules in others. To further complicate matters, some local municipalities also have access regulations. The time and money involved in managing conflicting regulations adds to developers' costs.

The players at different levels may have vastly varied and conflicting interests and positions. As we have seen, not having to charge sales tax gives e-commerce retailers a large advantage over traditional brick-and-mortar stores. The House helped the e-commerce industry by passing a five-year tax moratorium on e-commerce sales, and the Senate is expected to follow suit. The states are horrified, claiming massive revenue losses as a result. Proponents of e-commerce found a friendlier ear on Capitol Hill than they would have at any state capitol, and took advantage of it to try to preempt action at the state level.[18]

Whether you are playing offense or defense, you have to identify the right forums—local, state, federal, or international; legislative, regulatory, or judicial—in which to influence governments' rule making activities. It is also important to recognize that actions in different forums often interact, either to strengthen or to undermine efforts to shape the rules. You may, for example, seek to influence new legislation while preparing to influence its eventual interpretation by regulators, and to initiate court proceedings if necessary. Companies in established industries have long understood this. In comparing the attractiveness of federal and state venues for rule making, one government relations professional commented, "We have facilities in 38 states. If you are a large corporation, it is more efficient to deal with one big bureaucracy in Washington than 38 individual bureaucracies who all have their own little philosophical and political tendencies."

Principle 6: The Ability to Influence Rule Making Is a Weapon in the Competitive Game

Efforts to influence government are often a form of business competition in disguise. One observer has commented that regulators frequently ignore the accusations of a company's competitors, whose motives are questionable, but always listen to customers. This phenomenon generates a dynamic whereby companies work with their customers to influence the political process to the detriment of their competitors. How, for example, did the Justice Department come to file suit against Microsoft? "There's an industry out there that has a financial stake and a survival stake in the Microsoft case," one government relations professional has observed, "and my impression is that, being unable to beat Microsoft in the marketplace, they've picked another realm."

Customers and competitors of Microsoft helped trigger government interventions by filing their own lawsuits and lodging complaints with federal agencies. Customers, including companies such as Apple and IBM, came forward to complain about Microsoft's tactics. Competitors, like the browser developer Netscape, also sought to play the government-intervention card. In 1996, Netscape lodged a formal complaint with the Justice Department accusing Microsoft of providing subsidies to manufacturers who agreed not to install competing browsers and of offering some customers financial incentives to remove Netscape Navigator and replace it with Internet Explorer. Microsoft called Netscape's actions "a calculated attempt . . . to enlist government and media in its marketing campaigns."[19]

Or consider the response of independent bookstores to the proposed 1999 merger between retail book giant Barnes & Noble and the country's largest book wholesaler, Ingram Book Group. As the *Los Angeles Times* reported, "An all-out lobbying effort against the proposed deal, led by the American Booksellers Association trade group, swamped the FTC with letters and e-mail."[20] In this round in the competitive struggle between small independent businesses and megastores, organizing to influence government gave the mom-and-pop stores a weapon that proved decisive. Faced with likely opposition from the FTC, Barnes & Noble backed out of the deal.

A similar dynamic can develop between domestic businesses supported by the U.S. government on one side and foreign businesses supported by their own governments on the other. In mid-2000, for example, U.S. Trade Representative Charlene Barshefsky announced a telecommunications trade deal with Japan that would ostensibly "open Japan's telecommunications market to genuine competition." The deal required Nippon Telegraph and Telephone (NTT), the largest telecommunications company in the world and Japan's dominant provider, to cut connection charges to foreign carriers by $1 billion per year. However, experts predicted that the agreement would have little impact because of the close relationship that remained between NTT and the Japanese government. Although NTT had been restructured and its fixed line operations split in two, the government still owned a 53 percent stake in the holding company and the company had powerful allies in the Ministry of Posts and Telecommunications and the Legislature. NTT controlled 95 percent of Japan's fixed phone lines, operated Japan's leading Internet service provider, and held a 67 percent stake in Japan's most formidable wireless provider.[21] The company was using its monopoly profits to invest and compete abroad, for example, it purchased Verio, a Colorado-based high-speed data communications company in mid-2000. One consistent aim of the U.S. government's trade negotiations with Japan since the 1980s has been to put an end to this kind of practice, often at the urging of U.S. business.

These three cases exemplify a broader phenomenon: rule-shaping contests among businesses in the same industry, between different links in a value chain, and between competing industries. The rule making game often prompts companies to form coalitions to oppose the efforts of special interest groups. But businesses also compete among themselves to influence rule making. The bottom line is this: If you do not participate in making the rules, others may shape the playing field in ways that are disadvantageous to you. "If you don't do the work," says one CEO, "someone else will. And if you're not there, someone else will be there. And they may or may not represent your interests."

Efforts to influence government should be an integral part of business strategy for many, perhaps most companies. This is especially true when the basic rules of an industry are being created (as in e-commerce) or shifting dramatically (as in telecommunications). You cannot hope to be effective unless you actively involve government relations professionals in the development of business strategy.

Principle 7: The Influence Game Is Never Over

The rule making game does not have a beginning or an end. Engagements get won or lost, but the game goes on. Typically, it ebbs and flows, moving on to a new set of issues or a different forum or a different stage of the process or a different level of government. Thus the players must remain ever vigilant and not let down their guard. According to one experienced lobbyist, "The president can sign a document into law, and by the time the ink is dry somebody's already put in another piece of legislation to overturn it. So it is never ending." The Family and Medical Leave Act was defeated four times before Congress finally passed it in 1993. External forces can also suddenly bring an issue to the forefront: A series of school shootings in 1999 gave the gun-control lobby tremendous momentum and revived the issue of violence in music lyrics and video games.

Sometimes issues that have been resolved in one arena are reopened in another. For instance, the Bureau of Alcohol, Tobacco, and Firearms (ATF), a division of the Treasury Department, passed a regulation allowing wineries to include the following wording on wine labels: "The proud people who made this wine encourage you to consult your family doctor about the health benefits of wine consumption." Senator Strom Thurmond, whose daughter was killed by a drunk driver, immediately introduced legislation to ban such labeling, arguing that the wine industry was trying to link a dangerous product to a healthy lifestyle. Three weeks before resigning in 1999, Treasury Secretary Robert Rubin wrote to Senator Thurmond agreeing to reexamine the labeling issue. (Thurmond had been blocking three key Treasury Department appointments, which were confirmed the day he received Rubin's letter.) The wine industry had worked for several years to convince the ATF to allow the labels. But Strom Thurmond's passion on this issue led to a setback with potential long-term effects.[22]

Nor is there a statute of limitations on when things can change. For example, the Ohio legislature, backed by the governor, passed a sweeping tort-reform bill in 1996 to reduce the number of civil lawsuits and limit the damages awarded to injured parties. The bill was a huge victory for business and hospitals. Nearly three years later, however, the Ohio Supreme Court struck down the law as a violation of the state constitution. According to one Ohio businessman, "A lawsuit can put a company out of business just like that. And now that ominous threat is out there again."[23] Ohio businesses had believed that this threat had been laid to rest, but a different branch of government revived it.

"Only the paranoid survive," as Intel CEO Andy Grove so aptly put it.[24] Grove was referring to competition in the marketplace and the impact of disruptive technologies, but he could have been talking about competition to shape the rules imposed by government. If you are not vigilant, you can win some battles but lose the war.

Common Mistakes

Success in influencing government requires you to lay a foundation by defining goals, organizing internally, and building relationships with influential players. Then you have to craft specific strategies by identifying leverage points in government processes, building coalitions, and framing persuasive messages. The rest of this book provides the tools for doing so. As you proceed, keep in mind the following mistakes that novices make, which can seriously undermine your efforts.

Mistake 1: Lacking Clear and Realistic Goals

Many companies go to Washington because they think they should be there, but without a clear sense of why. "One of the biggest mistakes any company makes, small or large, is not doing a needs assessment before they approach the government relations concept," says one government relations professional. "They need to take a minute and ask 'What exactly do we need? How can we go about it?' They really have to spend the time to figure out what exactly they need—and how's the best way to get it. Not enough companies do that." You have to be pragmatic about what you can accomplish when you approach government. You are not going to change the world; you probably are not going to change your industry. But, if you develop a good strategy with clear, concrete, achievable goals, you might be successful. In order to do that, you must have goals that make sense for your business and that are congruent with the political environment. "You have to get to the point where you know what it is you want," says one Washington insider. "And you have to build a case about why that's valuable."

Mistake 2: Not Recognizing When to Shift Goals

Strategies must be flexible. However hard you work at articulating clear, realistic goals, circumstances will sometimes dictate that those goals have to shift. A change in the political climate can abruptly make this the wrong time to push for change. Thus you must be prepared to accomplish only some of your goals and to recognize when you have achieved all that you are going to. You also have to be prepared to shift your goals. Consider the tobacco companies, whose ability to market their product has been eroded by increased regulation. They have responded by constantly adjusting their approach to government and the public. When efforts to forestall government lawsuits failed, the industry responded by shifting to negotiation in order to shape the outcome.

Mistake 3: Not Being Ready to Play Both Offense and Defense

Your strategy will depend on what you are trying to accomplish and whom you are dealing with. You need to be ready to make proactive, offensive moves when your goal is to accomplish something specific, but you should also be prepared to react with defensive moves when someone threatens your position. You may find yourself playing offense and defense simultaneously, especially when you are pursuing multiple goals. Intel, for example, vigorously defended itself when the FTC was investigating its business practices. But it simultaneously attempted to forestall future problems by giving away some of its research in order to expand the overall market, cutting back on suits against new entrants in the chip industry and loosening its patent-licensing practices. Even as it looked to head off a broader antitrust suit by the FTC, Intel was working with allies at The Computer Coalition for Responsible Exports to press the Clinton administration to ease restrictions on powerful computers with potential military applications.[25] At the state level, Intel was in the forefront of a business coalition opposing a $1-billion-a-year income-tax cut due to appear on the ballot in Oregon, where Intel was one of the largest private-sector employers. The company was alarmed about the impact of a tax cut on education and other state services.[26]

Mistake 4: Not Having a Backup Plan

If your marketing strategy fails, you do not close up shop; you implement an alternate strategy. The same logic applies to strategies for influencing government. Be prepared for the failure of your initial strategy and have alternate plans ready. This is a lesson that WorldCom learned to its sorrow when antitrust regulators killed the company's proposed merger with Sprint. Lacking a backup plan, WorldCom was left vulnerable, itself a potential takeover target. At the same time, though, do not be too quick to give up on a strategy that did not work the first time. The rule making and refereeing climate is continuously changing, and as a result an approach that failed last year might work next year.

Mistake 5: Having Preconceived Notions about Allies and Adversaries

On any issue you know intimately, you will be able to predict with considerable accuracy which businesses and groups will be on which side. In most cases, you will be on target about your allies and adversaries. Sometimes, though, the unexpected will happen: companies and groups that should be on your side are not, and parties that should have no interest will strongly support your position. You should always be open to these possibilities. And, with such unexpected alliances in mind, battle with your adversaries on specific issues but do not alienate them—your opponent on this issue may be your best friend on the next one. As one professional lobbyist observes, "A very important rule is: Your partner today could be your opponent tomorrow and vice-versa."

Core Tasks

Once you acknowledge the capacity of government to influence and constrain your business, the next step is to begin to build the foundation necessary to be effective. What should you be trying to achieve? How should you organize your government relations efforts? What are the critical relationships you need to build? By setting goals, creating internal capabilities, and developing external relationships, you *lay the foundation* for success in influencing government.

Part I explores foundation-building activities in detail. Chapter 2 presents a framework for diagnosing the impact of government on your business and defining goals. Chapter 3 looks at how to design your governmental relations organization. Chapter 4 offers advice on how to build the relationships necessary to support your influence efforts.

Once you have a solid foundation in place, you will be ready to craft winning strategies to achieve your objectives by influencing rule makers and referees. Crafting strategies means identifying key leverage points in government processes, building coalitions, and framing persuasive messages. These elements of an effective influence campaign are explored in Part II. Chapter 5 explains how to identify key leverage points in government processes. Chapter 6 provides tools and techniques for mapping influence networks and building coalitions. Chapter 7 explores how you can frame persuasive messages to support your coalition-building efforts.

Finally, you have to anticipate how the game will change so you can stay ahead of the curve. Part III examines the future of the influence game, focusing on the impact of globalization and the Internet. Chapter 8 explores how skilled government relations professionals conduct "corporate diplomacy" in an increasingly boundary-less world. Chapter 9 looks at how the Internet is leveling the playing field for influence professionals.

PART I

LAYING THE FOUNDATION

When we asked the CEOs, government relations profession-als, and lobbyists we interviewed what it takes to be effective in influencing government, they spoke of three linked sets of capabil-ities. The first set is *diagnostic:* Can you diagnose government's potential impacts on your business and clearly define achievable goals? The second set is *organizational:* Can you build an organi-zation capable of linking government relations to business-strategy development and of designing and implementing strategies to in-fluence rule makers and referees? The third set is *relational:* Can you build relationships with key decision makers in government and those who influence them so that you will have relationship capital to draw on when you need it?

Defining Goals: What Influence Games Do You Need to Play?

Businesses cooperate in order to create economic value and com-pete to claim their respective shares. Experts in strategy have char-acterized this mix of cooperation and competition as "the games that businesses play."[1] Often these games involve government.

Governments establish, interpret, and enforce the rules of competition and cooperation among businesses. Governments also mediate between businesses and other interest groups such as consumer and environmental organizations that seek to restrict business conduct. To define your goals for influencing government, you have to figure out what games you need to be playing. Chapter 2 provides a framework for identifying how government rule making can affect your business and for developing goals.

Organizing to Influence: How Should You Organize Your Government Relations Efforts?

You cannot hope to have an impact on government decision making if you are not organized to influence. This means building your internal government relations capabilities, as well as tapping into key external sources such as consultants and lobbyists. Who should lead your government relations operation and how will they be involved in strategy formulation at the top? How will you staff your organization and where will it be located? How will you raise and deploy money to influence political processes? Chapter 3 provides guidelines for answering these and other essential questions about how to build your government relations capabilities.

Cultivating Relationships: With Whom Do You Need to Build Relationship Capital?

To succeed, you have to build a base of relationships with government decision makers. In conjunction with direct approaches to decision makers, you should think through who influences the influential people and build relationships with them, too. Once you have identified who is likely to be in key positions to affect the decisions you care most about, you have to get access to them and build some relationship capital. To do this, you need to draw on your employees internally and tap into external resources such as trade associations. Chapter 4 shows you how to do this.

Although the chapters that follow present these three tasks separately, they are inextricably intertwined in the process of laying a foundation for influencing government. Understanding what games you need to play and what goals you want to achieve is a necessary prerequisite to building the right organization. Effective efforts to build government relations capabilities help you to develop relationships. These relationships in turn will help you to stay on top of what is going on in key games and to respond flexibly to changing circumstances.

CHAPTER 2

Linking Goals to Business Strategy

Before you can begin to figure out how to influence government, it is essential to understand *why* you need to do so. The first task is to diagnose how government can help or hinder you in implementing company strategy. You also have to anticipate how others—other businesses and nonbusiness interest groups—might try to influence government to advance their own interests at your expense. "From the point of view of internal planning," one senior government official advises, "you need to understand how government affects your bottom line, and what that might mean in terms of what you do differently. Then you have to translate that insight into very concrete measures." As a prelude to deciding where to focus and how to exert influence, this chapter will help you diagnose the impact of government on your business.

How Could Government Impact Your Business Strategies?

It is important to diagnose business impacts carefully: Government can play so many roles in shaping business strategy that it is easy to get confused. Government's spheres of influence on business range from taxes and labor laws to antitrust intervention, patent rulings, and tax incentives. As one government relations professional points out, "The overriding point for companies of any size is that government impacts your ability to do business in a wide variety of ways. And you have to stay knowledgeable about what their impact is." Government intervention is sometimes a threat, sometimes an opportunity. It sometimes impacts the company's core strategies and sometimes merely imposes routine reporting requirements. A proposed change in public policy may affect just one company, or every firm in a particular industry or geographic area, or the entire U.S. business community.

Crafting Hybrid Strategies

Goals for influencing government should flow directly from the analytic frameworks that companies use to develop business strategies. As Michael Porter noted in *Competitive Strategy*, "No structural analysis is complete without a diagnosis of how present and future government policy, at all levels, will affect structural conditions."[2] Porter integrated the impact of government into strategy development by focusing on how it affected his "five-forces" analysis of rivals, potential entrants, suppliers, customers, and substitute products. More recently, however, strategy experts have deemed this approach inadequate. As Pankaj Ghemawat notes:

> The emphasis on folding non-market considerations into the analysis of market relationships tends to focus on the effects of non-market variables . . . at the expense of systematic analysis of their evolution, including efforts to *influence* them. More specifically, this approach steers attention away from the political processes whereby administrative policies are formed and implemented. . . . These difficulties are compounded by the typical simplifying device of ignoring the internal workings of government and treating it as a whole (albeit formless) entity.[3]

Previous efforts to develop frameworks for "nonmarket strategy" have explicitly dealt with government influences on business.[4] The nonmarket approach looks at the impact of government separately from the impact of market forces and then integrates the two. Though a step in the right direction, this approach suffers because the boundary between "market" and "nonmarket" is artificial and far from clear-cut.

We find it more productive to focus on the key types of games businesses play: *value-net games* and *public interest games,* both of which could involve governments as players. We further distinguish between strategies *to play the game* and strategies *to shape the rules.* Here too, efforts to shape, interpret, and enforce the rules may or may not involve governments in their roles as rule makers and referees.

The result, as illustrated in Figure 2.1 and elaborated in detail below, is a framework for developing *hybrid strategies*: strategies both for identifying and playing key games and for shaping the rules. The term *hybrid* emphasizes the need for businesses to develop strategies to both (1) play varied and potentially linked games and (2) shape the creation, interpretation, and enforcement of rules. To elaborate, the model rests on five conceptual pillars:

1. *Business strategy as game playing.* In the new lexicon of business strategy, companies participate in ongoing games in

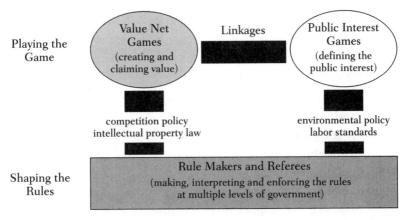

Figure 2.1 Hybrid strategies.

which economic value gets created and distributed.[5] Games are a useful metaphor because outcomes (market share, profits) in business are the result of interactions among the strategies of a set of players. The games businesses play involve a mix of cooperation to create value and competition to divide up (or claim) the value that has been created. Companies make moves as they play these games and these moves interact. They also seek to *shape the rules* in advantageous ways, for example, by undertaking a merger, or entering a new market.[6]

2. *Value-net games and public interest games.* We will focus on these two categories of business games, both of which may or may not involve government. *Value-net games* have to do with cooperation and competition among businesses.[7] *Public interest games* pit coalitions of businesses, and even entire industries, against nonbusiness organizations like unions, consumer groups, and environmental organizations.

3. *Governments as rule makers, referees, and players.* In both value-net games and public interest games, governments establish the rules by which the players operate, acting as *rule makers.* But governments also interpret and enforce the rules, effectively acting as *referees.* Governments may even participate directly as *players,* for example, as customers in value-net games or as initiators of policy changes in public interest games.

4. *Multilevel games.* Many influence games involve multiple interacting levels of government—local, state, federal, and international. Actions at one level can influence what goes on at other levels. Understanding these interactions is critical to devising good influence strategies.

5. *Linked games.* Many influence games also have both value-net and public interest components. A merger, for example, needs government approval; it may also elicit the opposition of environmental groups. Thus it is often essential to understand and manage linked games.

To diagnose the impact of government on your business, you will need to pinpoint the types of games in which you are involved, the roles governments play in these games, and the multiple levels of government that affect what you do. You may also need to anticipate and shape linkages between value-net games and public interest games. But first we need to digress a bit to define these types of games and to explore the roles that governments can play in them.

Value-Net Games

Games that businesses play with each other in the course of their ordinary activities take place within what Barry Nalebuff and Adam Brandenburger call the *Value Net*.[8] Companies seek to advance their goals by crafting strategies for cooperating and competing with other players in their value nets—customers, suppliers, competitors, and complementors. Figure 2.2 illustrates the value net,

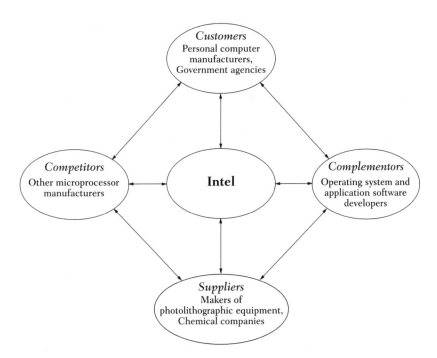

Figure 2.2   Intel.

using as an example Intel and the microprocessor-manufacturing game. As Nalebuff and Brandenburger explain:

> Along the vertical dimension of the Value Net are the company's customers and suppliers. Resources such as raw materials and labor flow from suppliers to the company, and products and services flow from the company to its customers. Money flows in the reverse direction, from customers to the company and from the company to suppliers. Along the horizontal dimension are the company's competitors and complementors. . . . A player is your complementor if customers value your product more when they have the other player's product. . . . A player is your competitor if customers value your product less when they have the other player's product than when they have your product alone.[9]

Intel, for example, buys raw materials and processing technology from many sources, and sells microprocessors to computer makers such as Compaq and Dell. The company competes with chipmaker Advanced Micro Devices and complements Microsoft's operating system and applications software.

Businesses cooperate to create economic value; they compete to distribute or claim the value that gets created. Consider, for example, a large manufacturer like Ford Motor Company. Ford cooperates with its suppliers to design new vehicles even as it negotiates vigorously with them over the terms on which parts will be supplied. By cooperating to develop new cars, Ford and its dealers and suppliers create a valuable pie of economic value. By negotiating over price, quality, and delivery terms, they divide that pie.

Changing the Game

The players in the value net continually seek to change the game to create and claim more value. While Ford and its suppliers work together to sustain their competitive advantage vis-à-vis competitors, they also try to transform relationships in the value net in advantageous ways. Ford carefully fosters competition among its suppliers and manufactures critical components in-house to ensure that the company does not become too reliant on a single source for key parts. As part of its strategy to change the game, Ford announced in 1999 that it would cooperate with General Motors and Daimler Chrysler to create a huge new electronic procurement exchange to leverage electronic transfer of data and reduce procurement costs. Its suppliers were understandably uneasy.

Strategy researchers have identified five classic strategies that businesses use to change the game within the value net: imitation, combination, shut out, entry, and hold up (see Table 2.1).[10] Understanding what roles, if any, governments play in efforts to change the game is an essential first step in developing an influence strategy.

Table 2.1 Five Business Strategies

Strategy	Description
1. Imitation	Companies seek to imitate others' successful products, processes, and systems while preventing imitation of their own.
2. Combination	Companies seek to increase concentration within their industry, and their own position in it, by acquiring or merging with other businesses. Competitors (and affected customers and suppliers) may seek to block these moves.
3. Shutout	Companies seek to have their own technologies accepted as standards, shutting out competing technologies. Developers of competing technologies engage in what Shapiro and Varian (1998) call "standards wars."[a]
4. Entry	Companies seek to enter new markets, either alone or in alliances or joint ventures. Their products or services may essentially duplicate existing offerings, or they may offer attractive *substitutes* based on different technologies. Companies whose markets are threatened attempt to exclude potential competitors and oppose their efforts to establish a beachhead.
5. Holdup	Companies seek to promote competition in their customer or supplier industries by encouraging the entry of new companies, development of substitutes, and fragmentation of upstream and downstream industries through contracting practices. Customers and suppliers seek to prevent being "held up."

[a] C. Shapiro and H. Varian. *Information Rules: A Strategic Guide to the Network Economy* (Boston, MA: Harvard Business School Press, 1998).

Governments as Rule Makers and Referees in the Value Net

Government rule makers and referees shape businesses' ability both to initiate and to defend against these strategies—to play offense or defense in value-net games. Specifically, the ability to make game-changing moves is constrained by laws and regulations governing competition, antitrust, intellectual property, product-approval processes, and technical standards. When governments review applications for mergers and acquisitions or hear legal cases concerning intellectual-property rights or takeover disputes, they are acting as rule makers and referees in value-net games between businesses.

Consider, for example, the debate about Napster, the online service for sharing digital music files. Napster triggered a firestorm of outrage in the music industry about piracy of music. The Recording Industry Association of America (RIAA)—the major-label trade association—with the rapper Dr. Dre and the heavy-metal band Metallica sued Napster for copyright infringement late in 1999. But it was unclear how intellectual-property law applied to such an innovation, so Napster's opponents also pursued a legislative remedy and persuaded key senators to hold hearings in the summer of 2000. A coalition of over 60 Artists Against Piracy—including Alanis Morissette, Hanson, and Bon Jovi—supported this effort. With financial support from RIAA, the National Association of Recording Merchandisers, Disney, Myplay.com, and the digital-rights management firm Reciprocal, Artists Against Piracy took out ads in major newspapers during the hearings. The results of the court case are still undetermined, but in November 2000, Napster took a step toward legitimacy by arranging a deal with media giant Bertelsmann AG to develop a legal version of the music-sharing service.[11]

Because governments can influence the outcomes of value-net games, many companies seek to involve rule makers and referees to gain advantage. Moves to influence government are commonplace when playing defense against others' strategic initiatives (see Table 2.2).

Table 2.2 Strategies and Examples

Strategy	Example
Forestalling Imitation: Businesses seek to protect their intellectual property from imitation through patents, copyrights, and trademarks and by designating critical information as trade secrets. Companies often turn to the courts to referee disputes over intellectual property.	Amazon.com filed a business methods patent for 1-click, a technology that stores credit card information and shipping preferences to enable customers to make online purchases with one click of a mouse. Amazon's competitor Barnes & Noble introduced similar technology it called Express Lane. Amazon sued for patent infringement. In December 1999, Amazon won a preliminary injunction barring Barnes & Noble from using the technology.[a] Speed and ease are part of the appeal of Internet shopping. Amazon gained some time to exploit its edge.
Blunting Combination: Businesses seek to prevent competitors' strategic combinations by raising antitrust questions or challenging deals in court. Sometimes businesses form coalitions with competitors, customers, and suppliers for this purpose. Even if they fail to kill the deal outright, antitrust authorities may demand substantial concessions in order to approve the deal.	In 1999, a coalition of local and national telecommunications companies, including AT&T and MCI WorldCom, successfully sued in U.S. District Court to prevent U.S. West from marketing the long-distance services of Qwest Communications.[b] The suit alleged that U.S. West's marketing of long distance violated the Telecom Act of 1996 because its local market wasn't sufficiently open to competition. Ironically, as a result of this suit, Qwest acquired U.S. West, a merger that received FCC approval in March 2000.
Winning Standards Wars: Governments can play central roles in standards wars. Sometimes winning a government contract to develop a new technology represents an inside track to establishing a technology as a standard. In other cases, governments may favor domestic standards over foreign ones or one domestic standard over another.	Qualcomm used a last minute lobbying effort directed at Chinese Premier Zhu Rongi to negotiate an agreement in late 2000 to develop a wireless network in China using its CDMA technology. This was a major step in its campaign to gain international acceptance for the CDMA standard in the face of stiff competition from the rival European GSM standard. Under pressure from the U.S. government, the Chinese Ministry of Information Industry initially appeared to agree to build a CDMA network, but support had vanished as political tensions rose between the United States and China. Qualcomm was ultimately successful, but both governments played major roles in the process. Both the United States and Europe had sought to link the dispute to Chinese admission into the World Trade Organization.[c]

(continued)

Table 2.2 Continued

Strategy	Example
Deterring Entry: Businesses seek to deter or delay competitors' entry into a market by calling on governments. Government may also prevent incumbent companies from taking actions to discourage the entry of new competitors.	In mid-1999, a coalition of mortgage lenders formed FM Watch, a high-profile lobbying group devoted to preventing Fannie Mae from expanding into commercial mortgage lending. Founders of FM Watch included Mortgage Insurance Companies of America; the Consumer Bankers Association; and the Consumer Mortgage Coalition, led by Chase Manhattan, Wells Fargo's Norwest Mortgage, General Electric's GE Capital, and PNC Bank's PNC Financial. Fannie Mae, which is private but operates under a government charter, responded rapidly and hired two well-known Washington lobbying firms—Williams & Jensen and Griffin, Johnson, Dover & Stewart—to oppose efforts of a coalition formed to pursue unspecified legislative or regulatory issues that may be opposed by Fannie Mae. When criticism began to intensify, Fannie Mae, Freddie Mac, the Independent Community Bankers of America (representing smaller lenders), the National Association of Homebuilders, and the Urban League formed their own lobbying group, the Homeownership Alliance, to oppose trends that would harm consumer access to the lowest cost mortgage options. On its Web site, the Alliance characterized FM Watch as "a group of large money center banks . . . seeking to spread unfounded fears about risks to the housing system."[d]
Preventing Holdup: Governments may act to prevent companies from "holding up" their customers or suppliers. Typically, the vehicle is antitrust review by the Federal Trade Commission, the Justice Department, or other agencies.	Cigarette wholesalers and distributors sued major tobacco companies in early 2000, charging them with illegally fixing prices. Tobacco companies defended their prices as competitive, but the suit alleges collusion to keep prices artificially high.[e]

[a] "Amazon.com Rival Hit with Injunction as Big Rush Begins," *National Post* (3 December 1999).

[b] "High Court Lets Stand FCC Veto of U.S. West-Qwest Sales Pact," *Dow Jones News Service* (28 February 2000).

[c] "Walled Out: For Qualcomm, China Has Beckoned Twice and Then Hung Up." *Wall Street Journal* (13 July 2000).

[d] "Fannie Mae, Freddie Mac Form Advocacy Group," *Wall Street Journal* (7 August 2000).

[e] "Tobacco Companies Are Sued by Distributors Over Pricing," *New York Times* (9 February 2000).

Sometimes businesses appeal to rule makers and referees not to win but to deter weaker players by disrupting or delaying their plans or imposing burdensome penalties. Delay is often a valuable side effect of government involvement in value-net games. Global Crossing, a small player in the telecommunications industry in 1997, has recently emerged as a major force in the long-distance fiber-optic cable market. One reason for its success is its savvy use of the government's refereeing function to slow down the competition. In November 1998, a consortium of 33 companies, including AT&T, British Telecom, and MCI WorldCom, applied to the FCC for a license to run a fiber-optic cable from Japan to the United States. Such approvals normally take about two months. Global Crossing, whose own fiber link across the Pacific was scheduled to begin service at about the same time, petitioned the FCC to delay approval of the cable and to investigate whether the consortium inhibited competition. The FCC finally approved the new cable in July 1999, and also announced that it would launch a broad inquiry into the undersea-cable business. Global Crossing's carefully constructed lobbying campaign earned it a six-month lead.[12]

Governments as Players in the Value Net

Alongside their roles as rule makers and referees, governments often function as players—customers, suppliers, competitors, or complementors—in businesses' value nets. When this is the case, it is important to think through the implications for your strategy, as illustrated in Table 2.3.

The government players involved can be state or federal, domestic or foreign—and all may influence matters. Procurement, for example, can be extremely political, particularly when dealing with governments in foreign markets. Consider the efforts of the Clinton administration since the mid-1990s to open up the way the Japanese government dealt out public works projects—worth more than $250 billion annually—to construction companies. Long-standing collusion between officials and the industry had discouraged competition and excluded outsiders from winning bids. Even after years of effort to open the market, U.S. companies

Table 2.3   Roles and Implications

Role	Implications
Customer: The government purchases everything from computer systems and jet fighters to paper clips and rubber bands. The federal government's purchases of goods and services from U.S. businesses total many billions of dollars annually.	If government is or could be a customer of your business, you should analyze carefully how its agencies purchase goods and services.
Supplier: The government supplies water and electricity to many businesses.	If your business buys commodities from the government, it behooves you to understand how it establishes prices and possibly to try to influence the pertinent regulatory processes.
Complementor: The government provides infrastructure, such as the transportation system necessary for the distribution of goods.	If your business relies heavily on the quality of a particular feature of infrastructure (such as roads or railroads), you should explore ways to get it upgraded.
Competitor: It is rare but not unknown for government agencies to compete directly with businesses. The U.S. Post Office, for example, competes with UPS and other companies to deliver parcels.	If your business is in competition with a state-controlled enterprise, it is essential to understand how it is governed and how its scope of activities can be influenced.

got only 0.02 percent of this work in 1999, less than one-tenth of the Japanese share of U.S. public works projects.[13] This was the case even though Japanese construction costs were estimated to average 3.5 times more than in the United States.[14]

Filling in the blanks in Figure 2.3 will serve as a starting point for thinking through which government entities play key roles in your company's value net.

Public Interest Games

Nonbusiness interest groups—environmental and advocacy groups, unions, and consumer organizations—often seek to persuade government to impose costs on business in the name of

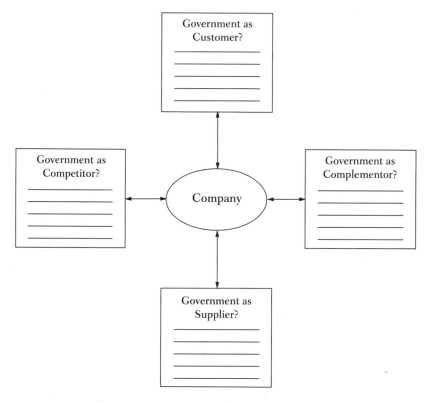

Figure 2.3 Company and government entities.

protecting what they assert to be the public interest. We have called contention over these efforts *public interest games* because they amount to a competition to define the public interest. Regulation, taxation, and subsidies are often the focus of such competitions, for example:

- DoubleClick, an Internet advertising firm that creates and monitors banner ads on Web pages, found itself at the center of a controversy over Internet privacy. The company tracks individual Web surfer's activities by monitoring which ads they click on, but maintains anonymity by assigning each user a number. In the fourth quarter of 1999,

DoubleClick completed a $1.7 billion acquisition of Abacus Direct Corporation, which marketed consumer-purchasing data to catalog firms. DoubleClick soon announced that it would sell information that combined its Web-surfing data with Abacus' personal data. This announcement alarmed privacy advocates, who sought government intervention, and triggered more than 100,000 customer complaints. DoubleClick was hit with six private lawsuits, an inquiry by the FTC, and investigations by several states. Its stock price dropped 15 percent.[15] In March 2000, the company backed away from the plan and its CEO admitted publicly, "I made a mistake."[16] The controversy led to negotiations between the FTC and Web advertisers, culminating in a July 2000 self-regulation agreement whereby the industry would develop and publish rules on customer profiling, and the FTC's Bureau of Consumer Protection would have the power to enforce them.[17]

- In late 1999, the Occupational Safety and Health Administration (OSHA) and the Clinton administration proposed new ergonomics standards aimed at preventing repetitive-stress injuries. The draft rules—the agency's fourth attempt to establish national standards—covered an estimated 27 million people who work on computers, on assembly lines, and in other jobs that require repetitive motions. The proposal included strict provisions triggering OSHA oversight of companies that incur high rates of such injuries and mandatory six-month light duty assignments for injured workers. A wide range of business groups organized to fight the rules, protesting that OSHA had grossly underestimated the costs to business of implementing the new rules and provided insufficient protection against fraudulent injury claims.[18] Several trade organizations banded together to challenge the science linking repetitive motion to injuries, as well as OSHA's economic estimates. A Cato Institute study argued that the field was so fraught with uncertainty and bad science that OSHA should abandon the standards.[19] In June 2000, the House of Representatives rejected an amendment to an appropriations bill that would have provided funding to OSHA to enforce the proposed rules.

- In early 2000, Wal-Mart, the country's largest retailer, faced a challenge from organizers for the United Food and Commercial Workers (UFCW) union. Wal-Mart employed 850,000 nonunion workers and had long fought unionization of its workforce. Now meat-department workers in Wal-Mart stores, in Jacksonville and Palestine, Texas, were the targets of UFCW organizing efforts.[20] The National Labor Relations Board (NLRB) declared them eligible for a separate union vote because of pay and skill differences between them and other Wal-Mart workers. When meat workers in the Jacksonville store voted to unionize, the company challenged the vote, but the NLRB upheld it. Workers at the Palestine store voted not to unionize, but the vote was disputed; it is likely to be appealed by the UFCW. After the Jacksonville vote, Wal-Mart announced that it would end meat-cutting operations in Jacksonville, Palestine, and 178 other stores in six states, a move it said was unrelated to the organizing efforts.[21] Union officials said the NLRB ruling meant that Wal-Mart would have to negotiate with the Jacksonville butchers before eliminating the meat-cutting department.[22]

- The U.S. Transportation Department issued proposed auto-testing regulations designed to reduce the risks of airbags. The auto industry largely supported the new rules, but opposed a severe crash test that would inflate an airbag forcefully enough to cushion an unbelted adult male crashing into a solid wall at 30 miles per hour. Surprisingly, groups ranging from the National Transportation Safety Board to the American Trauma Society also opposed the new crash test arguing that it could result in airbags that would cause injury in less severe accidents.[23]

Governments as Rule Makers and Referees in Public Interest Games

In public interest games, nonbusiness players like investor groups, unions, consumer organizations, and environmental groups form coalitions to influence government rule making. Because the resulting regulatory challenges typically affect whole industries, industry associations organize to counter the influence of non-business groups. Companies that are vigorous competitors in the value net often become close allies in public interest games.

Regulations are imposed because businesses can disadvantage or harm other constituencies. Examples include failing to report accurate financial results to investors, breaching consumers' personal privacy, permitting unsafe working conditions, selling dangerous products, and polluting the environment. Typically, those affected—investors, consumers, workers, and communities—then organize to influence government to control corporate behavior. In particular, they want governments to force businesses to meet specific requirements, such as financial-reporting requirements, bans on certain uses of consumer data, standards for workplace safety, and pollution-abatement measures. Government intervenes to prevent businesses from claiming value from other sections of society, in effect, protecting the public interest.

Governments also impose *taxes* on businesses to provide services that would not otherwise be funded, such as education, national defense, and basic scientific research. Taxes are necessary when reliance on market mechanisms will not result in socially efficient levels of investment in such services. The interest groups that benefit from these uses of tax revenue, such as teachers, scientists, and defense contractors, come to have vested interests in seeing investment in public goods sustained or increased. Again, they organize to influence the political process.

Governments may also single out particular industries for focused taxes or subsidies (including tax breaks) intended to alter supply-and-demand relationships for particular products and services. Cigarette taxes, for example, are intended to reduce demand for cigarettes and compensate for health-related costs. Subsidies for research and development, tax breaks for locating a plant in a particular community, or mortgage interest deductions are incentives intended to encourage specific behaviors. Business and nonbusiness groups often organize to support or oppose such taxes and subsidies. Consider, for example, ethanol subsidies, whose supporters range from the small farmers who grow corn to the large corporations that convert it into ethanol.

Governments as Players in Public Interest Games

As in value-net games, government agencies are not just rule makers and referees in public interest games: they sometimes are independent players with their own agendas. Early in 2000, for example, the National Association of Insurance Commissioners, which represents state insurance regulators, proposed a set of universal standards for every state to apply in regulating insurance companies. Insurance companies have long been regulated state by state, requiring them to get dozens of approvals for each new rate or product. This circumstance put them at a disadvantage relative to federally regulated competitors, such as banks and securities firms. State insurance regulators expected insurance companies to take advantage of legislative changes allowing them to merge with banks and securities firms, which would result in larger companies with the power to press for a single federal regulator. The state insurance regulators' proposal was an effort to preempt this development and retain their authority to regulate. The consensus at the time was that, without such changes, state regulation was doomed.[24]

It is essential to keep in mind that government officials sometimes pursue independent agendas and build coalitions to support them.

How Value-Net Games and Public Interest Games Differ

Value-net games and public interest games both involve cooperation and competition among players to influence the making and interpretation of government rules. In both, as illustrated in Table 2.4, governments can operate as rule makers, referees, and/or players.

However, there are important differences between these two types of games. Value-net games tend to be played by individual businesses and ad hoc coalitions. As an example of the latter, consider the companies allied against Microsoft. Netscape helped to organize an anti-Microsoft coalition called Project to Promote Competition and Innovation in the Digital Age (ProComp). Companies and trade associations supporting ProComp include Corel, Netscape, Oracle, Software Publishers Association, Sun Microsystems, Sybase, and worldweb.net. ProComp's Web site offers "A User's Guide to Microspin in the case of *U.S. vs. Microsoft*" and a forum for people who fear reprisal to confidentially report anticompetitive actions by Microsoft.[25]

Public interest games, by contrast, tend to be played between industries, represented by their industry associations, and

Table 2.4   Government Roles

	Government as Rule Maker	Government as Referee	Government as Player
Value-net games	Legislatures pass laws concerning competition policy and intellectual property. Regulators translate legislative intent into rules.	Regulatory agencies rule on mergers, and courts make decisions on intellectual-property rights.	Governments are customers, suppliers, competitors, and complementors of businesses.
Public interest games	Legislatures pass laws concerning environmental protection, privacy, worker safety, and taxation. Regulators translate legislative intent into rules.	Regulatory agencies decide whether to grant permits and enforce compliance with environmental and worker safety regulations.	Legislators and regulators pursue independent agendas in attempting to define the public interest and to initiate or block change.

coalitions of nonbusiness organizations. A classic example is environmental groups' efforts to get tougher fuel-economy standards applied to sport-utility vehicles over the opposition of the auto industry.

Governments also tend to play different roles in the two types of games. In value-net games, government usually functions mostly as referee: Agencies and the courts interpret and enforce antitrust regulations and intellectual-property law. The role of government as rule maker—creator of new rules and regulations— tends to be more prominent in public interest games than in value-net games; the legislature is usually involved and the games are more political. The players in public interest games are trying both to shape the rules and to influence how they are interpreted and enforced.

Exceptions to this general rule arise when the structure of an industry is changing in fundamental ways. The impact of the Internet on issues such as intellectual-property protection is one example. Another is the sweeping change in the telecommunications industry initiated by the Telecommunications Act of 1996, to be discussed in Chapter 5.

Multilevel Games

Both value-net and public interest games are often played at multiple, interacting levels of government. As the state insurance regulators' effort to preempt federal regulation exemplifies, participants may seek to influence one level of government to block or shape action at another level. "Sometimes you need to get out of Washington," one government relations professional counsels. "Sometimes you need to go to the states and do it. If the noise level is too high inside the Beltway, then get out. Focus on where the major operations of the company are. Deal with the governor and state legislature or the local Republican or Democratic party. If there are too many competing interests, concentrate on the outside."

Some games continue to be played at multiple levels over the long term. The U.S. tobacco industry, for example, has fought a multilevel battle to avoid regulation and liability for the health consequences of smoking. In 1992, the U.S. Supreme Court opened the door to suits by smokers alleging that cigarette companies had hidden the health dangers of smoking. In 1994, shortly after executives of all the major tobacco companies offered sworn testimony before a congressional committee that they believed nicotine not to be addictive, leaked internal documents from Brown & Williamson revealed that the industry had extensive knowledge of tobacco's risks. This revelation spawned a series of state lawsuits, beginning with a suit filed by Mississippi, to recover public health expenditures for treating smokers. In 1996, the FDA announced its intention to regulate tobacco; the legal challenges by the industry ultimately resulted in a 5 to 4 Supreme Court decision that the FDA lacked the requisite authority. In the meantime, efforts to negotiate settlements with the states faltered but ultimately led to a $206 billion settlement with 46 states. In late 1999, the U.S. Justice Department sued the industry to recover billions of dollars the federal government had spent on medical care for smokers. In mid-2000, a Florida jury imposed compensatory damages of $12.7 million and punitive damages of $144.9 billion in a class-action suit filed by ill smokers. The Florida verdict is being appealed, but defeats such as these may in turn spur a settlement at the federal level.[26]

Multilevel games can involve interactions between the national and international levels. In 1998, the United States and the European Union officially recognized each other's inspection, testing, and certification requirements for a number of traded products, codified in Mutual Recognition Agreements (MRAs). The MRAs affected nearly $50 billion in traded goods in multiple sectors, including medical devices. The U.S. medical-device industry strongly supported the MRA process through its trade group, the Health Industry Manufacturers Association (HIMA); the industry's support of MRAs was part of a larger strategy to pressure the Food and Drug Administration to streamline its approval process for medical devices. By working at the international level, in other words, the industry made progress at the federal level. While it is rare in standards-disputes cases for a domestic industry to ally itself with a foreign government's position, this example illustrates the value of thinking flexibly about how to advance your position.

Clearly, it is essential to think through how actions at various levels of government could interact, and to keep track of what is going on at the various levels. Your intelligence gathering should focus not just on the issue at hand but also on the potential for action at multiple levels.

Linked Games

Value-net games and public interest games often get linked. Mergers and acquisitions—classic moves to change the game in the value net—usually require the approval of government regulators. But they may also call for efforts to win the approval of nonbusiness groups, such as environmental watchdog organizations. If you do not anticipate who might take an interest in such moves, it is easy to be blindsided. Failure to understand and manage linkages can lead to big problems, as the following examples illustrate.

The Federal Trade Commission (FTC) and three western states sought in 1999 to block a proposed merger between BP Amoco and Atlantic Richfield Company (Arco) that would have created one of the world's largest oil companies. The FTC was alarmed that the combination of the number-one and number-two oil producers, both major landowners in the natural-resource-rich North Slope of Alaska, would give the new company too much pricing control. The FTC was also influenced by the lobbying efforts of advocacy groups like Greenpeace and the U.S. Public Interest Research Group, both worried about the environmental impact of the proposed merger on the sensitive regions of Alaska. This linkage seriously complicated efforts to consummate the merger. Ultimately it proceeded, but only after the FTC sued to block the deal and BP Amoco agreed that it would sell Arco's Alaskan oil holdings.[27]

The passage of the Telecommunications Act of 1996, which will be discussed in detail in Chapter 5, provides another example of the impact of linkage. The debate centered on the future of competition in the industry, and involved a vigorous contest for influence between long-distance companies such as AT&T, MCI WorldCom, and Sprint and regional bell operating companies (Baby Bells) such as Bell South and Ameritech. But this value-net game got linked to debate over the Communications Decency Act of 1996, which restricted minors' access to indecent content on the Internet. This public interest game pitted Internet service providers (ISPs) and civil-liberties advocates against social conservatives. Ultimately, both the Telecommunication Act and the Communications Decency Act passed, but the Supreme Court struck down the latter as unconstitutional.

Linkages between value-net games and public interest games can create both threats and opportunities to advance your interests. For example, a proposal in early 2000 by the U.S. and British governments to make the human genome part of the public domain sent tremors through the biotechnology industry, which is counting on future profits from gene patents. In a single day, spooked investors withdrew tens of billions of dollars in market value from the industry. The governments' intent was to promote cooperation between a British group and an American company to finish mapping the genome, which could have immense public health benefits. The full fallout of this government action remains to be seen, but this attempt to define the public interest could have significant implications for value-net games in the biotechnology industry.

It is essential to trace potential linkages early on and then to take steps to manage them proactively. Otherwise, you can be caught flat-footed.

Identifying the Key Games

Every company is influenced by government regulation, in forms such as labor laws, safety standards, and taxation. But figuring out what games you need to play and what roles governments play (or could play) in these games naturally depends on your company and your industry. Governments play prominent roles in most businesses' value-net games, but they are particularly important when

(1) industry structure is changing in fundamental ways and (2) companies seek either to enter new markets or to defend themselves from strategic challenges by other businesses. Public interest games primarily concern industries with a significant impact on public health and safety, such as oil, chemicals, tobacco, pharmaceuticals, automobiles, and, increasingly, collection and use of consumer data. But some games, like those involving employee benefits or privacy on the Internet, potentially affect all businesses.

To jump-start this process, take a few minutes to list in Table 2.5 the most important value-net and public interest games your company is currently engaged in, specifying the key players, rule makers, and referees, actual and potential. Also think about potential interactions among levels of government and linkages

Table 2.5   Goals

	Players	Rule Makers	Referees	Level(s) of Government
Value-net Game 1				
Value-net Game 2				
Value-net Game 3				
Public interest Game 1				
Public interest Game 2				
Public interest Game 3				

between value-net and public interest games. At what levels (local, state, federal, international) is this game played, or could it be played? At which one or two of these levels are you most likely to achieve your goals?

Defining Your Goals

Once you have identified the key games you need to play, you can define your goals for each. Are you going to play offense or defense? What is your time frame for having an impact? How will you know if you are successful? It is essential to develop clear and achievable goals.

Are You Playing Offense or Defense?

Are you promoting changes in the rules (offense) or seeking to prevent changes (defense)? Initiating change is a much tougher proposition than blocking a change supported by others. Generally speaking, blocking a change means preserving the status quo, and inertia is a powerful force to have on your side. "Blocking something is a lot easier than starting something," observes one professional lobbyist. "It takes a lot less energy and time to block something than it takes to build momentum to get something done. Anything new, or any change, takes a lot of resources, energy, and time."

If you are playing offense, the tasks before you range from framing the case for change to garnering support to sustaining momentum over the long haul. Historically, major changes in the rules like the Telecommunications Act of 1996 have taken years to bring about. It took consumer and labor groups seven years to get the Family and Medical Leave Act signed into law. You will have to develop strategies that are sustainable over time.

Are You Trying to Block, Shape, or Delay Change?

If you are playing defense, are you seeking to block changes outright, to shape the rules to harm you less, or to delay the inevitable? Different goals demand different strategies, for example:

- *Blocking change* is your goal if the change in question will seriously damage your business.

- *Shaping change* is your goal if the rules are clearly going to change but you can influence how they are written.

- *Delaying change* is your goal when support for change is too widespread to block it and shaping efforts are pointless because any version of the change will harm your business.

You need fallback plans, too. If you cannot accomplish your primary goal, what is your next-best option? Look for signs that you need to shift goals. For instance, it may make sense to shift from shaping to blocking if the proposed changes are taking a form that would be harmful to you. If you stick too unbendingly to one goal, you may overlook an opportunity to minimize damage or even gain advantage. Microsoft, for example, stuck to protesting the unjustness of the antitrust case against it instead of trying to influence the Justice Department's actions.

For each game you need to play, take time to fill out Table 2.6.

Table 2.6   Achieving Goals

Goals: What are we trying to achieve?

Time frame: What is our time frame for having an impact?

Responses: How is the opposition likely to respond to our moves?

Measures of success: How will we know we have been successful?

Designing Your Government Relations Operation

The framework presented in this chapter gives you a basis for (1) thinking about the most important strategic games your company needs to play; (2) identifying the other key players; (3) assessing government's roles as player, rule maker, and referee; (4) figuring out at what level(s) of government the games are being played; and (5) identifying and managing linkages. But the best strategy in the world cannot be implemented—or even developed in the first place—without the right infrastructure supporting government relations in your organization. How will you organize internally to project influence externally? This is the subject of Chapter 3.

CHAPTER 3

Organizing to Influence

There is no one right way to organize your government relations efforts. How you choose to do it will depend on the nature of your business, the size of your company, your goals, and the availability of resources. This chapter provides you with a framework for making critically important organizing choices based on a thorough diagnosis of your needs.

Organizing Questions

A fundamental message that bears repeating at the outset is that you cannot hope to have an impact if your top executives do not believe that influencing government is a priority and do not invest accordingly. As one government relations professional observed, "If there is a group of people in America who don't really understand the political system, it is corporate executives . . . I've spent a lot of time meeting with people in the business community who, if they took over a chain of fast-food restaurants, would never do it without learning everything they could possibly learn about the fast-food business. But they make no real effort to learn about the impact of politics on their companies."

So the starting point for organizing to influence is to devote the necessary resources, the scarcest and most important of which is senior management time. The example for doing this must be set at the top. As one CEO put it, "You've got to go personally and spend some time [in Washington]. You have to carve a chunk out of your schedule to go ask people for advice and counsel, to find out what you don't know."

Beyond that, there are certain organizing questions you have to answer. Your choices will set the stage for all that follows:

- Who will you select to head your government relations functions?

- Where will government relations fit in your organization's reporting structure?

- Where will you physically situate your government relations resources?

- Will you use consultants, employees, or a combination?

- How will you mobilize your employees?

- Should you establish a political action committee (PAC)?

- Should you make soft-money contributions?

Who Will You Select to Head Your Government Relations Function?

The biggest question you face when deciding who should head your government relations function is whether to choose someone internal who is familiar with the challenges facing your business, or someone external who is familiar with the inner workings of political and regulatory processes (Table 3.1). Skilled government relations professionals and lobbyists make good arguments in support of either choice. "If you decide to hire somebody under the government relations function," one said, "that person should be an expert in government relations, not necessarily an expert in

Table 3.1 Hiring a Head of Government Relations—Questions to Ask

Do you understand the major government related issues facing our organization? Do you understand the overall government relations strategy of our company?

Do you understand the major strategic and operations goals of our organization? Can you become familiar enough with our markets and technologies to offer good advice?

What experience do you have dealing with legislative issues? Regulatory issues? What experience do you have in Washington and/or the state capital?

If our company has global operations, do you have the skills to direct company efforts to influence foreign governments?

your industry. You need somebody who understands the rules of the game in Washington, DC." Another saw it differently: "I would appoint an internal person if I had a good, savvy one." In fact, people from either background can be successful, but only if they are the right people (see Table 3.2).

Table 3.2 Backgrounds of Heads of Government Relations

1. *Domestic Industry Association Background*

    BA in Political Science

    Worked for a member of a Congressional committee for two years

    Spent 10 years as vice president in charge of government affairs and public affairs at a trade association

    Helped lead a broad-based industry trade association seeking regulatory reform for two years

2. *International Affairs Background*

    BA in Economics and MPA in international relations

    Legislative assistant to a U.S. senator for two years

    Spent four years as an International Trade Specialist, Office of Japan, U.S. Department of Commerce

    Director, Global Strategy and Analysis at a manufacturing industry association for four years, directing work in Japan and Asia

3. *Legislative and Regulatory Background*

    BA in Public Administration and Economics

    Ran a number of political campaigns for members of Congress

    Chief of Staff to two members of Congress

    Worked in several committee-staff capacities for members of the Senate

    Assistant Secretary in U.S. Department of Health and Human Services

    Vice President of Strategic Management at a health-care consulting firm

Whichever way you decide to go, keep in mind that the key success factor in this job is the ability to act as a bridge between the worlds of business and government. The best heads of government relations are capable of quickly grasping the ways that government affects your business. They can communicate effectively to people on both sides of "the abrasive interface" of business-government relations. As one head of government relations expressed it, "You need someone who will get in and get to know the issues. Someone who knows people. Someone who will develop rapport with the operating people in the company—to know what they want."

You should also seek a good match between the particular influence challenges facing your company and the capabilities of the person you select for the job. If the issues facing your company are highly technical and regulatory in nature, you may choose someone who is familiar with the relevant technologies and markets. On the other hand, if you anticipate having to push or block legislation, you may want to hire someone who has an in-depth understanding of legislative maneuvering.

Many firms rely entirely on outside lobbyists and consultants for their government relations needs. This can be a logical choice if your influence needs are minimal. It can, however, prove to be very expensive and, if you are not careful, not terribly effective. The tradeoffs associated with using outside consultants will be discussed in detail next.

Where Will Government Relations Fit in Your Organization's Reporting Structure?

How government relations fits into your reporting structure communicates, both internally and externally, the level of importance you attach to this function. Many government relations executives report to the general counsel. Inevitably, this positioning gives the function a more legalistic cast and a less central role than if they were to report to the CEO or COO. But it can make sense if most of the issues call for day-to-day dealings with regulatory agencies. In our survey of Fortune 100 government relations professionals, there was an even split between those who reported to the CEO and the General Counsel, respectively. Very few reported to executives further down the corporate ladder.

If influencing government is a core strategic goal, however, the head of government relations needs to be a full member of the senior management team. One high-level lobbyist advised, "I highly encourage everybody to have the government relations person very much involved in the corporate structure. That doesn't mean the person can't be an exmember of Congress who knows relatively little about business, but it means that that person has to be totally integrated into the company." Another said, "You need to be able to get results, and going through a corporate bureaucracy is every bit as difficult as going through a government bureaucracy. You need to have the access to the top person. Many corporations house government relations within the office of the general counsel. Those that are truly successful have them reporting to the chairman and CEO." A government relations professional echoed this point: "Many companies do not include their government affairs office in their inner circle. They get reports from government affairs on a regular basis, but they don't have the kind of give-and-take of engaging together in building the strategy or identifying the issues."

The bottom line is: If you believe that your company will make frequent attempts to influence government policy—whether those attempts are offensive or defensive, legislative or regulatory—your government relations function should be tied directly to the highest level decision-making structure of your company (Table 3.3). Many decisions will need to be made quickly; the fewer levels that

Table 3.3 Organizing Your Government Relations Function—Questions to Answer

To whom will the head of government relations report? How often will they meet?
What role will the head of government relations have in strategy development? In top-management team decision making?
How will the work of government relations, media relations, and advertising be coordinated?

have to be navigated, the better. One head of government relations described the process at his company this way: "The commitment of management goes all the way through. We talk policy at senior management meetings. We have a public policy steering committee that is comprised of our chairman, our president, CEO, our general counsel, our chief financial officer, and our senior vice president of corporate resources and myself. We meet quarterly to really assess our objectives and fine tune our strategies. . . . We have meetings at the senior level and then manager level on a regular basis. There is always a public policy component of those meetings."

If, on the other hand, you will need to influence government infrequently—and if, as mentioned previously, your interactions will primarily be with regulators—the government relations function could be located lower down the hierarchical ladder. Remember, though, that even if you mount large-scale campaigns infrequently, decisions will still need to be made quickly. The ability to act quickly is *the* key difference between successful and unsuccessful companies and associations.

If you choose to place your government relations function outside the normal flow of senior management decision making, be sure to provide key government relations people with mechanisms for quickly accessing the decision-making structure when necessary. Otherwise, the results will be incoherent or tardy. You may even miss opportunities altogether, because public policy decisions get made without input from your government relations staff and because your government relations staff will not lack the necessary stature when building key external relationships.

You also should assess how government relations will be integrated with your media-relations and advertising functions. These are all top-level corporate staff functions, usually are run by different senior-level people. But media relations and advertising are indispensable tools in the influence game. Tight coordination is essential. The best companies assign cross-functional project teams of professionals drawn from government relations, media relations, advertising, and the legal staff to run high-level influence campaigns. They also assign clear responsibility, usually to the head of government relations, for quarterbacking the overall effort in consultation with the senior management team.

Where Will You Physically Situate Your Government Relations Resources?

Your choices here are to situate government relations operations within corporate headquarters, in Washington, in state capitals, or some combination. Global companies also typically assign dedicated staff in overseas offices to follow government affairs locally. You should think about where your priorities are and place your people accordingly.

You should base these decisions on an analysis of available resources and influence needs. If you expect interactions with the Congress or state legislatures to be intermittent and occasional, it may well be workable to operate the government relations function from the corporate headquarters.

If your need for interaction will be more frequent, it may require a permanent presence. It is wise to have a presence in the capital city—international, national, and/or state—year-round if you want to be a player and have the necessary resources. One government relations professional observes:

> You have to make a real commitment to be responsive on a regular basis . . . there are a lot of competing voices out there and if you are going to play a role, you have to be heard. It doesn't always mean the loudest voice—it should be a steady input.

Another concurs:

> It is hard to run government relations from outside Washington. I know some professionals who do it, but it is very difficult for them to keep up and be a real player. For instance, I might get a call offering me a chance to meet with staff on the Senate Finance Committee at

5 o'clock and I am able to do it. Those opportunities are very valuable and don't come along every day. If I were at headquarters, I could never do it.

Of the respondents to our survey of Fortune 100 companies, 73 percent had an office in Washington with an average staff of nine professionals.

An on-site presence allows you to continually monitor the activities of Congress, the legislature, and the relevant regulatory agencies and to respond quickly when necessary. You can keep an ear to the ground much more easily if you are present than if you rely on information gathered by others. In the arena of governmental relations, nothing is truer than the maxim "forewarned is to be forearmed."

You do not necessarily have to expend a lot of resources to establish a Washington presence. You can start small and build incrementally. A leading medical devices company, for example, opened its Washington office about five years ago. The company, which has a strong government affairs focus, started with just one person in Washington. Its strategy was to let the company and the Washington representative get a feel for their roles and relationships and to slowly add staff once a clear need was identified. Today, the office has three professionals and is widely acknowledged as one of the most effective in its industry.

Suppose you conclude that you need to have an impact in a particular political center—state, national, or foreign—but do not have the resources to fund an on-site presence. What can you do? First, you hire someone good to run government relations at corporate headquarters, ideally someone who already has good relationships with the relevant rule makers. Then you let that person spend a lot of time travelling.

Second, you get involved with trade associations that provide effective early warning and coordinate the activities of their members. Keep in mind when doing this that some associations are much more effective than others. Your government relations people should make some hardheaded assessments about where your resources are best devoted.

Third, you need to think through how and when you will work with consultants.

Will You Use Consultants, Employees, or a Combination?

Next you need to decide whether your government relations staff should consist of people employed directly by your company, outside consultants, or some combination. Here again, there are pros and cons to each approach, and you may decide to customize your staffing issue by issue. For example, you may have a full-time internal staff but also hire professional lobbyists to deal with specific issues on a project-by-project basis. Ninety-seven percent of the respondents to our Fortune 100 survey reported that they routinely hire consultants for government relations operations (Table 3.4). A majority used consultants for targeted projects or employed a strategy of keeping a few consultants on retainer and then hiring others for specific projects. Only 13 percent of our respondents relied exclusively on consultants to represent them.

Your decision should be based on a straightforward assessment of costs and benefits. Professional lobbyists can be quite expensive, but so can a full-time staff with salary and benefits. If you anticipate needing personnel only a few times a year, it may be more cost-effective to pay consultants retainer fees than to maintain a full-time staff.

Table 3.4 Hiring Outside Consultants/Lobbyists—Questions to Ask

What past experience do they have in Washington/the state capital?

What past experience do they have in your industry?

How can they help you improve your relationships in Washington/the state capital?

What are their connections, legislative and regulatory?

Who are their other clients?

Are there potential conflicts of interest?

What examples of successes can they offer?

But cost has to be balanced against efficacy. Professional lobbyists are likely to already know who the key players are, where the leverage points are, and what potential obstacles exist. In most cases, they will already have built a base of relationships that allows them access. Your staff will catch up on these things, but doing so will take time you may or may not have. Consultants can be very helpful in charting strategy and helping you gain access. As one head of government relations expressed it, "A good lobbyist not only has the ability to assess the issue and how it affects your company, he knows what everybody else is thinking about it, doing about it—or has good relationships with those people so he can find that out."

An outside consultant may not understand the nuances of how a given issue impacts your company. More seriously, the fact that consultants are hired guns can undermine your company's message and goals. According to one government relations professional who refused to use professional lobbyists:

> The reason we don't hire consultants to help lobby is that the consultant supporting me today could be sitting across from the same member or staffer tomorrow supporting someone else on a completely different issue. I don't have any control over that. I feel it is important to convey that my company and I really believe in what we are lobbying for, and that we are not just there saying something because we are being paid to say it.

If you choose to hire outside lobbyists while maintaining a staff, you will need to think carefully about how the two will interact and clearly delineate the responsibilities and goals of each. You also face the same internal decision-making issues with outside consultants as you do with staff. Either they will need the autonomy to make necessary decisions quickly or mechanisms should be in place for them to quickly access your decision-making structure.

Close coordination and clear instructions are especially important when lobbyists are conducted real-time negotiations on your behalf. As one government relations professional expressed it, "Lobbyists do more than just put forward the company's view. Hopefully they get a chance to negotiate—for example, to fix a problem or agree to language in a bill. When it is time to negotiate, your representative needs to have the authority to negotiate for you. If he or she has to run back and get an opinion on everything, you are likely to get behind. When the process moves, it moves fast. You better be able to keep up with it."

How Will You Mobilize Your Employees?

Your employees are a priceless resource in your efforts to influence government. They have a direct stake in the success of your company. Even unionized workers often share public policy goals with management. You may differ with them on issues like liberalization of international trade and investment, but be of like minds when new competitors threaten to enter the company's markets. But employees must be organized if you are going to mobilize their influence.

Involving the Workforce

In part, this means straightforward efforts to educate employees about the issues. Caterpillar, for example, stamps a destination on each of its products early in the production process to remind workers of the importance of international trade. As one professional lobbyist put it:

> In most corporations there are from 5 to 15 percent of employees who will take an active role in government, write their congressman and do those sorts of things. So you've got a core of employees that would probably want to participate in politics. You have to develop an educational process to help them get over the fear and feel empowered. There's an even larger number who would participate in local activities like Boy Scouts and Rotary and those kinds of activities that are less political but still community-building stuff. You have to encourage that at the local level. If your company is known

as a company that encourages people to get involved, then you're going to have eyes and ears everywhere, you're going to have people who are willing to participate, who are willing to look out for the company's interests.

Educating employees means having a Web site and possibly a newsletter that alerts them to the key issues at the federal and state levels. It means using e-mail to provide information on potential impacts in terms that are directly pertinent to employees: "If this law is passed, it is going to cost us 8,000 jobs. . . ." The key is to bring home what goes on in government so employees can see the impact on their company, and therefore on their lives. By showing employees how they can affect government decisions, you can open up a whole new avenue of influence. You get a good return if 10 to 15 percent of your employees actually do something on a sustained basis.

Technology is available to support such efforts. There is software, for example, that enables management to provide information on government relations issues to employees electronically to help them write letters to the right decision makers. Such technology can also be used to mobilize customers and suppliers. In doing this, naturally, you have to be sensitive to corporate culture. But if you can develop a relationship of trust, it can be very effective. As one head of government relations put it, "The danger is that you will insult their intelligence. And you can do that quite easily by asking them to do something that they don't understand, by not giving them the information they need to make good choices and take intelligent actions. Other dangers are to go to the well too often and to exaggerate what you're trying to accomplish."

You also have to be very careful, lest you lose credibility with legislators. One senior congressional staff member recalled an "astroturf" (fake grassroots) incident during the debate over the Telecommunication Act of 1996: "I was working for a member of Congress, and we got bags full of material. But when we called to follow up on some of it randomly, the people had no idea what had been sent in their name. . . . There was a little bit of a backlash on that one."

But the right letter campaign can have an impact, especially if your goal is to delay or derail legislation. Recalled one former congressional staff member:

> You can influence the atmosphere under which legislation goes forward. For example, there was the Conservation Re-investment Act, a classic fast-track piece of legislation with all the environmentalists signed on to it. But then there was a grassroots backlash in the House from some conservatives and private property folks, especially out West. There was a fair amount of mail and constituent concern, some of which was organized. And while the bill still passed the House, it is bogged down simply because there is this atmosphere of distrust that did not exist before.

Leveraging Your Facilities Managers

Managers of the company's dispersed network of facilities are a particularly important group to organize. One professional lobbyist put it this way:

> If you think from an internal grassroots point of view, plant managers are the top of the pyramid. So you can't do anything that doesn't start with them. You need to make sure that they are educated, that they are treated as a class in and of themselves.

Another said:

> The plant manager is the guy in the congressman's hometown who ought to be going in to visit with him on a regular basis. And if you've got a key issue, the plant manager can go in and talk about an issue in a way that you can't relate in a letter or a phone call or an e-mail. The plant manager is also the one that can keep the policymakers educated as to what your company is all about, what you make, where you export it, where your sales are, what's the status of your employees, and whether or not they ought to have a minimum wage increase, those kinds of things.

To do this well, plant managers have to (1) understand that government relations is a core part of their job, and (2) be trained to manage contacts with government officials deftly. As one head of government relations expressed it:

> We tell plant managers: We want you to get the congressman or members of his staff out for a plant visit once or twice a year if you've got a new product or new service to demonstrate. If you've just planted 500 trees for the local Lions' Club, then you want to ask the congressman to get the assistant secretary of conservation in. There are all kinds of things you can do to keep yourself visible and keep yourself familiar to the member of Congress, state legislators and governors, and local officials. If a policymaker is familiar enough with what you do for a living, then something's going to come up, and the first thing on the policymaker's mind is, "Now how's this going to affect the XYZ company? This sounds like this could be trouble for them. I'd better call Ralph and find out before I commit myself here to my colleague." A member of Congress is on a trip over in Japan, and happens to be in a meeting with the Japanese Chamber of Commerce, and hears something. If the policymaker is conscious of what you do and how you do it and who you are, then there are all kinds of benefits you can derive from that.

Facilities managers need and deserve to be schooled in the kind of communication that works with government officials. This means getting them to be brief and to focus on the two or three key specifics that are going to affect the business most. The essentials can be taught effectively in short three to five-day programs on managing government relations. These programs can also provide opportunities for government relations staff to meet facilities managers, and hence further develop the internal coordination network. Finally, they are a way to communicate the importance of contributing to the company's political action committee.

Should You Establish a Political Action Committee?

Not necessarily—many companies do not—but PACs do perform a useful function. Money matters: every two years, members of the House of Representatives must run for re-election; every six years senators must do the same thing. To run and win takes money. Despite the argument that it is wrong for "special interests" to try to influence outcomes, the donation of money represents an essential, legal channel for people in business to help candidates who support their positions on issues that concern them. Political action committees (PAC) were established as a political reform, a means of allowing people to contribute in an effective yet regulated manner. It is often in your interest, and in the interest of your employees, customers, and community, for you to raise and deploy funds to help shape the composition of Congress and state legislatures. If you do not, others, who might not share your goals, will—to your detriment. As one head of government relations expressed it:

> I think PACs are important. I think it shows that we understand the system. We understand that it is not easy to get elected. We understand that people have to work very, very hard to raise the funds that are needed. And if we're not willing to help the people that we think should be here, we can only expect so much back from them.

A CEO who is active in public affairs echoed this sentiment:

> The corporate PAC is a very valuable tool for the guy who sits in Washington, because he is going to be asked all the time to participate . . . When the chairman from committee X comes around, and the staff is organizing a fundraiser of some kind, and the answer is, "Sorry, we don't have a PAC and we don't contribute," it is going to set you back.

This is, of course, a very positive view of how money can be used in politics. Obviously, the nation has a strong interest in ensuring that legislators are not "bribed" to vote in ways they might not otherwise have voted. And it would not be in the national interest if only people with a great deal of money could influence the composition of legislatures. But neither of these principals diminishes the right of citizens to help determine who will represent them and hence what laws will be passed.

Some of the advantages of establishing a PAC have to do with external effectiveness and some with perceptions within your company of the importance of influencing government. The pros of establishing a PAC include:

- PACs make you a player in the political process.

- Regular contributions keep your senior employees invested in the political process that may in turn help mobilize them when necessary.

- PACs help keep supportive officeholders in positions of influence in government.

- PACs increase your ability to gain access to decision makers.

There are also downsides to having a PAC. Some executives complain about constant pressure from legislators to contribute to their re-election campaigns. Some have complained that these requests amount to virtual extortion, especially when they come from officeholders that can affect the company's well being. You can protect against this pressure by not establishing a PAC. But that decision may also constrain the ability of the company to help determine who will sit in key legislatures. And it may not be all that helpful: Legislators seeking re-election may simply seek contributions directly from company executives.

You also have to evaluate carefully whether a PAC is the most cost-effective use of scarce resources. According to one top-tier Washington lobbyist, "The influence of PACs has gone completely down from what it was. The use of media has become far more effective. . . . It is getting more cost-efficient to target media that policymakers listen to, watch, or see." So you have to decide where you are going to get the most bang for your buck. One CEO also questioned PACs' effectiveness: "We don't have a PAC and we don't give soft money. I don't think a PAC actually buys you anything. We've had absolutely no trouble with access. We can say we gave everybody the same; we gave everybody nothing."

If you decide to establish a PAC, you then have to determine how to operate it. The rules are laid out in the Federal Campaign

Finance Law and administered by the Federal Election Commission.[1] The regulations govern everything from fundraising and making contributions to record keeping and methods of communication with politicians.

In addition to following the rules, you need to develop a strategy for solicitations and contributions. Who will be solicited and how? Who will the money go to and why?

When soliciting, your efforts are best directed at the top few tiers of management. When it comes to contributions, it is not practical to give money to everyone who asks. Ideally, contributions should be made only to legislators favorably inclined toward positions the company supports. As one former CEO put it, "It is perfectly okay to say we only support people who support us. There is nothing wrong with that. I'm not going to give money to somebody who consistently votes against our interest."

Some companies contribute to well-positioned incumbents or challengers in the hopes of getting access to that legislator. Some even give to both sides in a political race in the hope of being favorably remembered by whichever candidate wins. Each company, and each company executive, must think about ethics and effectiveness in making these decisions. But keep in mind that politicians have long memories: The winner will remember that you contributed to his or her opponent. Remember too that there are far better ways to gain access to a legislator. The best source of access is often through constituents.

How much should one contribute to a candidate? In a federal race, the maximum allowable contribution is $5,000 in the primary and $5,000 in the general election. As a general rule, however, $5,000 contributions are rare and tend to go to candidates engaged in tight contests for critical decision-making positions. More typical contributions to individual members of Congress are in the range of $500 to $1,000.

To see how contributions to law makers get distributed, take a look at the contribution profiles for the chairman and ranking minority member of the House Commerce Committee (Table 3.5). Given the range of business interests before this committee, it is not

Table 3.5   PAC Contributions to the Leadership of the House Commerce Committee, by Industry, 1999–2000 (as of June 1, 2000)

Industry	Contributions to Thomas Bliley (R-VA), Chairman	Contributions to John D. Dingell (D-MI), Ranking Minority Member
Agribusiness	$ 22,500	$ 13,500
Communications/electronics	62,399	69,931
Construction	5,000	3,000
Defense	5,000	4,000
Energy and natural resources	17,667	92,675
Finance, insurance, and real estate	84,968	43,300
Health	26,500	33,000
Lawyers and lobbyists	7,750	28,500
Transportation	19,000	24,015
Miscellaneous business	14,250	24,015
Labor	0	62,000
Ideological/single-issue	2,886	10,150
Total	$267,920	$411,691

Source: Center for Responsive Politics, www.opensecrets.org.

surprising to find contributions from a broad range of industries. The largest contributing industries—finance and telecommunications—reflect the many rule making challenges they are currently facing. Extensive data of this kind is available on the Web from organizations such as Common Cause (www.commoncause.org) and the Center for Responsive Politics (www.opensecrets.org).

A deeper look at PAC contributions to these two law makers by telecommunications firms and associations reveals some interesting patterns (Table 3.6). Chairman Bliley's contributions come from a coalition consisting of the long-distance companies and the small rural telecoms. Representative Dingell's support, by contrast, comes from the Baby Bells and urban and smaller regional players. Why might this be the case? Not surprisingly, it reflects key alignments that shaped telecommunications policy, including the crucially important Telecommunications Act of 1996. We will

Table 3.6 Individual PAC Contributions by Telecommunications Companies to the leadership of the House Commerce Committee, 1999–2000 (as of June 1, 2000)

Contributor	Contributions to Thomas J. Bliley	Contributions to John D. Dingell
Sprint	$3,650	$ 0
MCI WorldCom	2,750	0
AT&T	5,000	2,000
National Telephone Co-Op Association[a]	1,000	0
Winstar Communications	1,000	0
Cellular Telecom Industry Association	1,000	0
Comcast Corp.	5,000	3,000
National Cable Television Association	4,999	0
Verizon Communications	5,750	15,000
Ameritech Corp.	0	10,000
BellSouth Corp.	0	3,500
SBC Communications	1,000	3,000
U.S. Telecom Association[b]	0	1,000
Frontier Corp.	0	1,000
AirTouch Communications	0	1,000
U.S. West Inc.	0	500
MediaOne Group	0	1,000

Source: Center for Responsive Politics, www.opensecrets.org.

[a] Represents small, often family-owned rural telephone companies (for a list of members, see the Web site 207.197.132.133/pacs/gaveamnt/1998/00004473.htm).

[b] Represents primarily local/urban telephone companies and smaller regional companies such as Frontier and Alltel (for a list of members, see www.usta.org/fullmem.html).

look in detail at this legislative process and how it was influenced in Chapter 5.

These patterns suggest that a typical medium-sized company can hope, at most, to make a modest contribution to each or a number of supportive candidates. If yours is such a company, you should target your resources at key races in locales where your company has a strong physical presence and at helping supportive candidates attain or retain decision-making positions on key committees. You should also coordinate your donations as you do your other lobbying efforts. Note too that trade association PACs can help to advance company goals.

Should You Make Soft-Money Contributions?

No discussion of the impact of money on U.S. politics would be complete without a look at soft money, the unregulated funds that go directly to political parties to support "party-building" activities during federal elections. The sums involved are substantial. Total soft-money contributions to the two major political parties rose from $141 million in the 1995–1996 election cycle to over $256 million in 1999–2000 election cycle and the growth shows no sign of abating. (For contributions by industry and by party, see Table 3.7.) The magnitude of particular industries' contributions correlates closely with the potential impact of the federal government on these industries, especially if we adjust for industry size.

Similarly, there are few surprises in Tables 3.8 and 3.9 showing the largest donors to each of the major parties. Double giving of soft money to both Democratic and Republican committees is common practice among the largest and most heavily regulated companies. Common Cause reported that 81 donors gave $50,000 or more each to both parties during 1999.[2] The top 15 of these donors are listed in Table 3.10.

Are contributions of soft money a good investment? The contributors obviously believe they are advancing their interests, and anecdotal evidence suggests they are right. American Financial Group/Chiquita Brands, the insurance-and-banana conglomerate controlled by Carl Lindner, for example, contributed a total of $820,000 in soft money in 1999, the latest in a series of contributions by Lindner and related donors totaling over $3 million between 1995 and 1999. The company's principal political interest was the so-called "banana war" between the United States and Europe over European restrictions on bananas grown in Latin American countries. Few U.S. jobs were at stake, but Chiquita's Latin American interests were damaged. Through a concerted lobbying

Table 3.7 Soft-Money Contributions by Industry, 1999 versus 1995

Industry	1999	1995
Securities and investments	$ 8,203,313	$ 4,468,201
Telecommunications	6,266,514	3,290,975
Real estate	5,112,371	2,518,653
Transportation	5,010,491	1,430,842
Insurance	4,941,819	3,017,734
Pharmaceuticals and medical devices	4,275,610	1,898,320
Computers and electronics	3,780,902	1,037,860
Banks and lenders	3,736,484	1,459,425
Oil and gas	3,572,625	3,125,742
Entertainment and media	3,438,228	2,609,795
Electric utilities	3,040,278	1,080,975
Gambling	2,918,146	776,750
Retail	2,815,320	1,118,590
Aerospace and defense	2,349,358	1,534,600
Miscellaneous business	2,213,688	629,290
Food and grocery stores	2,048,568	1,166,000
Manufacturing	1,983,347	1,521,750
Tobacco	1,950,166	2,801,496
Health	1,847,714	1,752,301
Beer, wine, and liquor	1,554,807	1,050,007
Agribusiness	1,395,000	1,245,750
Metals and mining	1,284,158	572,700
Engineering and construction	1,226,605	1,010,155
Chemicals	1,152,895	1,118,950
Accounting and consulting	847,985	651,784
Automotive	780,213	570,275
Forest and paper products	721,675	447,250
Machinery	627,500	125,000
Tourism and lodging	607,300	344,695
Environmental and waste services	383,770	603,500
Textiles	240,652	562,000
Restaurants	229,100	216,000
International trade	120,000	694,270
Total Business	*$80,676,602*	*$46,451,635*

Nonbusiness Contributors	1999	1995
Trial lawyers	$ 2,751,337	$ 1,215,500
Lobbyists and DC lawyers	854,240	759,286
General practice lawyers	1,155,270	718,660
Labor unions	6,913,928	2,206,900
Political/ideological groups	1,586,559	395,900

Source: Common Cause, www.commoncause.org.

Table 3.8 Top Overall Soft-Money Donors to Republican Party Committees (January 1, 1999 through December 31, 1999)

Donor	Soft Money
Philip Morris Companies, Inc.	$922,067
AT&T	761,908
United Parcel Service	608,559
American Financial Group	550,000
Dominion Resources	513,378
National Rifle Association	478,100
Atlantic Richfield Co.	456,250
Microsoft Corp.	446,913
Richard T. Farmer, Chair and CEO, Cintas Corp.*	445,000
Freddie Mac*	410,000
Welsh Carson Anderson & Stowe	400,000
Enron Corp.	345,775
Pfizer, Inc.	337,446
SBC Communications, Inc.	335,553
Federal Express Corp.	330,350
Mirage Resorts, Inc.	310,000
Citigroup, Inc.	304,745
Union Pacific Corp.	300,960
Kojaian Management Corp.	300,000
Schering-Plough Corp.	293,500
The Limited, Inc.	290,750
UST, Inc.	289,603
American Airlines	284,089
Bell Atlantic Corp.	283,854
First Union Corp.	276,421

Source: Common Cause, www.commoncause.org.

*Totals do not include contributions from executives and/or affiliates.

campaign, Lindner managed to propel the banana issue to the top of the Clinton Administration's trade agenda, drawing on bipartisan support from Senate leaders Richard Gephart and Bob Dole.[3] The United States successfully brought a case in the WTO against Europe. *Time* magazine reported that the day the banana case went

Table 3.9 Top Overall Soft-Money Donors to Democratic Party Committees (January 1, 1999 through December 31, 1999)

Donor	Contributions
American Federation of State County and Municipal Employees	$1,405,000
Communications Workers of America	1,175,000
Service Employees Intl. Union	818,250
Aviation Products Management	561,000
AT&T	555,350
Peter L. Buttenwieser, President, P.L. Buttenwieser & Associates*	517,500
Sheet Metal Workers Intl Association	470,854
Intl Brotherhood of Electrical Workers	462,500
Ness Motley Loadholt Richardson & Poole	420,200
Williams Bailey Law Firm LLP	415,000
Peter G. Angelos, Attorney; Owner, Baltimore Orioles	400,900
S. Daniel Abraham, CEO, Thompson Medical Co.*	400,000
Microsoft Corp.	351,250
Milstein Group	343,389
Saban Entertainment, Inc.*	337,000
Bernard L. Schwartz, Chair and CEO, Loral Space & Communications*	335,000
Ian M. Cumming, Chair, Leucadia National Corp.*	325,000
American Federation of Teachers	321,000
Jon S. Corzine, Former Chair and CEO, Goldman Sachs*	320,000
M.A. Berman & Co.	315,250
Shorenstein Co.	315,198
Nix Patterson & Roach LLP	300,000
Louis Weisbach, CEO, Ha-Lo Industries, Inc.*	291,344
Learning Co.	291,000
Carl Lindner, Chair, American Financial Group/Chiquita Brands Intl.*	270,000

Source: Common Cause, www.commoncause.org.

* Totals do not include contributions from executives and/or affiliates.

to the WTO, Lindner contributed $550,000 to the Democrats, mostly through less-examined state party accounts:

> You wouldn't know how grateful Lindner was by checking records at the Federal Election Commission; he gave the Democratic National Committee (DNC) only $15,000 in the final 15 months of

Table 3.10 Double Givers (1999 Contributions to Both Major Parties)

Donor	Democrats	Republicans	Total
AT&T	$555,350	$761,908	$1,317,258
Philip Morris Companies, Inc.	86,641	922,067	1,008,708
American Financial Group	270,000	550,000	820,000
Microsoft Corp.	351,250	446,913	798,163
Atlantic Richfield Co.	170,000	456,250	626,250
Dominion Resources	110,150	513,378	623,528
SBC Communications, Inc.	266,150	335,553	601,703
Enron Corp.	223,250	345,775	569,025
Mirage Resorts, Inc.	253,621	310,000	563,621
Freddie Mac*	150,000	410,000	560,000
Federal Express Corp.	225,228	330,350	555,578
Citigroup, Inc.	221,450	304,745	526,195
American Airlines	185,000	284,089	469,089
Bell Atlantic Corp.	151,350	283,854	435,204
Anheuser-Busch Co., Inc.*	188,256	242,200	430,456

Source: Common Cause, www.commoncause.org.
*Totals do not include contributions from executives and/or affiliates.

the campaign. Instead, DNC officials instructed Lindner to give directly to state party coffers, which are subject to far less public scrutiny than federal-election accounts. On April 12, 1996, the day after Kantor asked the WTO to examine Chiquita's grievance, Lindner and his top executives began funneling more than $500,000 to about two dozen states from Florida to California, campaign officials told *Time*. The only record of the contributions is in often-remote state capitals, like Cheyenne, Wyoming, where contributors are not even required to list their employers. A Democratic official said the state party route was reserved for "hot potatoes"—donors who wanted some anonymity.[4]

In May 2000, Congress passed "carousel" legislation imposing rotating tariffs on European goods in retaliation for European refusal to abide by WTO rulings, reportedly after strong lobbying by Lindner.

Some companies refuse to play the soft-money game because they perceive its effects to be corrosive. Their argument is that it amounts to buying influence and that it has resulted in an escalating soft money "arms race." But many companies that have stopped making direct soft-money contributions still end up giving large unregulated sums—because they believe they have an impact. General Motors, for example, became the first of more than 30 major corporations to voluntarily stop making soft-money contributions in 1997. "It is the principle," GM's vice chairman, Harry J. Pearce, said in announcing the decision. But GM made "in-kind" contributions to the 2000 Republican National Convention with an estimated worth of over $1 million. The company provided 400 Cadillacs, sport utility vehicles, and minivans for use by organizers. GM also hosted two lavish lunch receptions—one for the Speaker of the House, J. Dennis Hastert of Illinois, and one for Lawrence B. Lindsey, the chief economic adviser to the presidential campaign of Governor George W. Bush of Texas.[5]

So should you contribute soft money? The escalation of soft-money donations has made it inadvisable for small and even medium-sized companies to do so. You simply cannot have an impact on your own. However, trade associations and other coalitions can be effective ways to pool contributions in order to have an impact.

In the end, the choice of whether or not to make soft-money contributions is as much a moral and ethical one as it is a question of business effectiveness. Critics have complained, with some justification, that soft money effectively circumvents the intent of campaign-finance laws and gives the richest donors disproportionate impact on the composition of Congress and the outcome of presidential elections.[6] But as long as the laws permit such contributions, and as long as competing interests make substantial contributions, the case for doing so will remain a strong one—if you can afford it.

Making Government Relations Accountable

If you do a good job of answering the key design questions outlined in this chapter, you will be well on your way to building an effective government relations operation. Now you have to be sure to stay involved and—crucially—to set clear goals and measure the results. The old management chestnut "You can't manage what you don't measure" is as true for government relations operations as it is for any other core business process. In fact, it is a common mistake to treat government relations as something that can not be measured. One government relations professional succinctly pointed out the inaccuracy of this attitude: "I'm in business development in the public sector." Another emphasized the importance of goal setting and measurement:

> You need to be bottom-line-oriented. You can't just accept the fact that the environment is difficult [for achieving goals]. My boss sets goals for me at the beginning of the year: Fix at least two major problems in Asia. It used to drive me crazy. What if I can't fix them? But it seems that if somebody really is on your back to get something done, you can show progress. You just have to change your mindset from "I will make my meetings, I will go on my visits, and I will dot my Is and cross my Ts," to "Oh, my gosh, I'm being held accountable. What have I done for these people?"

Measuring results, in turn, means setting realistic goals in the first place. Whatever the issue, you have to understand how it will affect your bottom line and what you would have to do differently. Will it add jobs or eliminate jobs? Is it going to affect your sales? Are you going to have to move?

The same measurement yardsticks should be applied to consultants. With consultants, remember that access does not necessarily equal influence. Consultants may be able to schedule meetings with high-level people, but meetings do not guarantee that you will have an impact. Do not let consultants cite meetings with decision makers as a measure of their effectiveness. When hiring consultants, press them for examples of situations in which they have had a measurable impact. As one lobbyist put it, "I think about the value I have been able to bring in terms of saving resources. You have to get to the bottom line, because I think there is a lot of that missing in Washington." Like every other facet of your government relations strategy, you need to set clear goals for consultants and regularly assess their impact.

In your dealings with industry associations too, you should set clear goals and hold their feet to the fire. You are making an investment and you are entitled to a return. It is essential to let your association know what you need and expect—for example, that you want it to be a reliable source of early warnings. Then make it clear that you will regularly reevaluate your continued membership. As one head of government relations put it, "Sit down and say, "Well how helpful has this been? I have given them so much money and what's happened? Was it something that was going to happen anyway?"

Making It Happen

To pursue a successful influence strategy, you have to organize to influence. You cannot just decide that you want to influence government action and expect to be successful instantaneously. Just as you need to work to define your goals, you need to develop a strong organizational structure that will allow you to achieve your goals. Once you have answered the questions posed in this chapter and started to put the organizational components in place, you will be in a strong position to develop relationships.

CHAPTER 4

Cultivating Relationships

Relationships are the foundation on which everything else rests. Like personal capital, you must invest time and resources to build up relationship capital so you can draw on it when you need it. Accumulating relationship capital means more than just cultivating relationships with key people inside and outside government; it also means being able to mobilize these relationships when you need them.

Building the Base

If you wait until the last minute to try to influence key decision makers, you will have no base of relationships and hence no credibility. This is a mistake that novices often make, comparable to introducing yourself to your neighbors when your house is burning down. "You should meet people before you need them," says one experienced government relations professional. "It is ridiculous to go in and see them for the first time and expect them to immediately get down to substance on something that you've got. There's no foundation." A professional lobbyist echoed this saying, "The biggest mistake CEOs make is that they don't think they need any-thing here in Washington. You don't go to Congress when you are in trouble. You've got to build up to it."

Relationships that provide a foundation for exerting influence must be painstakingly built; they cannot simply be bought when you need them. It is easy, though expensive, to hire a high-powered lobbyist to represent you in times of trouble. But it is hard to realize value from such an arrangement (and even to know if you are getting value) without good relationships of your own. "People have a knee-jerk reaction: You have a problem, you have to hire a lawyer or a lobbyist to solve the problem," says one high-profile lobbyist. "That can often be the worst thing to do."

It may seem extravagant for top management to invest time in building relationships with people in government before you have a specific goal in mind, but rest assured, it is not. Consider the costs of not having a solid foundation of relationships in place. If an issue that could impact your business suddenly appears on the agenda in Congress, will you be able to move expeditiously to in-fluence the process? Failure to respond effectively to a single major governmental challenge can be far more costly than years of judicious investment in relationship building. As Microsoft and others have found to their sorrow, once you are behind the curve, it is hard to play catch-up.

The right network of relationships also helps you to anticipate problems and to prevent them from becoming full-scale crises. In-telligence gathering is an important function of your relationships with people in government: The best information about what is going on is not available from the media or on the Web. It can only come from people who are enmeshed in the day-to-day flow of public affairs. Relationship building has a defensive function as well as an offensive one.

To illustrate the importance of relationships, consider the dif-ferent approaches adopted by Intel and Microsoft in their respec-tive antitrust cases. As we saw in Chapter 1, these two companies took very different stances when faced with antitrust investiga-tions. Microsoft regarded government with contempt and had largely avoided dealing with Washington except when absolutely necessary. Not until 1995 did Microsoft reluctantly open a small office in Washington. By the time of the Justice Department investigation and subsequent suit, Microsoft's resentment of government had bred a matching resentment of its own. Since Microsoft had not invested in laying a foundation, the company's relationship capital was very low.

Microsoft spent a great deal of time and money playing catchup by hiring expensive lobbyists and trying to build last-minute relationships, a campaign that was viewed by many as a desperate attempt to make up for past mistakes. Microsoft even went so far as to use the few relationships it had built with Washington State politicians to try to cut the federal budget allocations for the Justice Department's antitrust division. The company's moves were described in the following way in a *New York Times* editorial:

> Microsoft argues that its multimillion-dollar lobbying campaign and donations have been defensive, an effort to counter large lobbying campaigns by its rivals to spur the Justice Department into action. The company charges that Justice officials have themselves overstepped the boundaries by suggesting to foreign governments that they also go after Microsoft, a charge denied by the department. Microsoft has every right to mount its best arguments in court and the public arena. But using its money and power to undercut a legitimate regulatory function of the Justice Department ought not to be the way Microsoft pursues its interests.[1]

Intel had a much more developed relationship with the FTC. "Intel has a legislative affairs department based in Washington, and that group has grown in a lot of areas," says a former regulatory official. "They have a very large lobbying presence, not just because of the FTC but for other reasons too." Intel worked with regulators and legislators long before the antitrust issues arose, and had built up relationship capital in key places.

Both cases involved issues of credibility, and in the final analysis Intel had quite a bit while Microsoft had none. Intel's case was settled with little fanfare and essentially no harm to the company. Microsoft is facing potential breakup. Many factors contributed to the divergent outcomes, but one key factor was relationships (or lack thereof).

Principles of Relationship Building

As you construct a relationship building plan, keep in mind the following general principles:

- *Cast a wide net.* Eventually your efforts at influence may focus on specific decision makers. But in the meantime, think about all the individuals who might be in positions to influence the outcome of issues facing your company, such as committee chairs, party leaders, and regulatory heads. Then think about who potentially influences those decision makers, such as other committee members, committee staffers, individual members' staffs, and technical staff. One way to start is simply to identify which of a key legislator's staff members are responsible for specific issue areas. As you accumulate this information, you should begin to draw some maps of who influences whom.

- *Approach relationships as a two-way street.* Intel had credibility with the FTC in part because the company had helped the regulatory agency over the years. As one former regulatory official points out, "Government officials are always dealing with people who need something. All the time. If you are calling to offer them something, you are building up credit in the bank so that you can use it later on." The need to reciprocate is a very strong social norm. So doing favors is a potent way to gain influence.[2] To the extent that you help other people solve their problems, you can expect (within limits, of course) to draw on them to help you.

- *Be prepared to spend some money.* Political contributions help make you known and keep you visible. You should therefore seriously consider setting up a Political Action Committee (PAC) to make contributions to supportive lawmakers. This serves the dual purpose of building relationships and keeping in office elected officials who share your perspectives and goals. Keep in mind, though, that contributions are only part of an overall relationship-building strategy. As one professional lobbyist put it, "A lot of these guys who have a lot of money have great access, and they have the ability to make their case in a very important and influential way. But in the end, policymakers have to make their decision on whether or not what they are voting for is good public policy." Contributions may help you get access, but access does not equal influence.

- *Assess potential relationships in light of your goals, not party affiliations.* Try to find and develop relationships with influential people—decision makers and those who influence them—who are sympathetic to your goals, regardless of their affiliation. Focus on the individuals, not the parties. It can be dangerous to be too closely tied with one political party. "You have to be careful in the political arena," one government relations professional warns. "Some people are too aligned with one party, and that's a mistake." At the same time, you should recognize that some key decision makers are not going to be sympathetic. Here you have to decide whether they are convincible, or implacably opposed. If the latter, the best you can do is to try to build a sufficiently powerful coalition to overcome their opposition.

- *Leverage internal and external resources.* As we said in Chapter 3, relationship building is not something that only you and your Washington representative or senior government relations person can do. Think widely about resources and contacts inside and outside your company who can help bring you and your concerns to the attention of decision makers. We will discuss this point in more detail later in this chapter.

Finally, remember that credibility is hard to build, easy to lose, and sometimes impossible to regain. People in government are just that—people. If you mislead them, presume too much, or put them in an untenable position, they will not forget it. "Washington really is a small town," one government relations professional comments. "If you present your side of the story with any inaccuracies, with any information that will not stand the test of the light of day, you may win the battle, but ultimately you will lose the war." A reputation for integrity is something to be husbanded and not squandered.

Influence Mapping

The first step is to clearly identify which relationships are the important ones and to establish priorities. Relationships with key legislators and regulators are crucial, but they are not everything. You also need to do *influence mapping* to figure out who has influence over those decision makers.[3] "Often the members themselves don't have a clear opinion on how they are going to vote," one lobbyist explains. "They depend on other people, particularly other members whom they trust, to either sway them or to tell them 'This is why it is good.'" Decision makers are embedded in networks of influence and information sharing. Understanding established patterns of deference will help you decide whom to approach, and in what order, to build momentum.[4]

In doing influence mapping, you should focus on:

- *Staff members, within both Congress and regulatory agencies.* Decision makers often rely on staff to be their eyes and ears and to brief them on the particulars of complex issues.

- *Other members of Congress.* Over time, because of interest and committee membership, legislators develop individual areas of expertise. Other members often defer to peers who are recognized as having good judgment on a given set of issues.

- *Generous party supporters.* Relationships between donors and those to whom they contribute are often a fertile source of influence channels.

- *Public interest groups.* These groups will have established relationships, both good and bad, with rule makers and referees.

- *Other businesses and industry groups.* Often you can leverage your efforts by linking up with like-minded business leaders who have their own relationships with government officials.

The key is to identify who defers to whom on issues of importance to you. Often it is useful to map these relationships graphically in the form of an influence network diagram (Figure 4.1). A diagram can be especially useful when you are trying to coordinate the activities of many members of a coalition, because it provides a common map from which people can work. The direction of the arrows indicates who influences whom, and the width of the arrows indicates the extent of their influence. In this case, three people influence the Committee Chair: an influential staffer, a respected member of the committee, and the majority leader of the

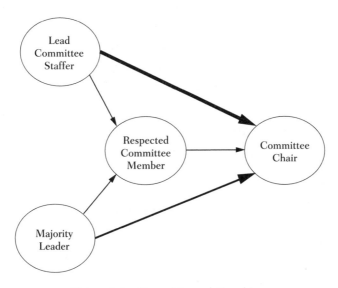

Figure 4.1   Committee relationships.

governing party. But there also are indirect paths of influence; both the staffer and the majority leader have influence over the respected committee member. This analysis suggests that it may be advantageous to approach the staff person and then the respected member before approaching the Committee Chair. In this way, you can exploit patterns of deference and meet with people in a promising sequence in order to build momentum. We will discuss these and other approaches to coalition building in detail in Chapter 6.

Conducting a Relationship Audit

The guidelines presented provide you with a basis for establishing relationship-building priorities. Given the games you need to play, what are the key relationships you need to develop? What is the current state of those relationships? What actions will you take to develop them?

To conduct a *relationship audit,* answer the following questions using Table 4.1 to organize your answers:

Enhancing Existing Relationships

- What are your existing relationships with rule makers (both legislators and regulators) and referees?

- What are your existing relationships with those who influence key decision makers?

- What is the strength of each of these relationships on a scale of 1 to 10?

- What might you do to improve some of these relationships?

Developing New Relationships

- Are there significant gaps in your relationship network, given the challenges you are likely to face in the next year or two?

- What new relationships have the highest priority for you?

Table 4.1 Key Relationships

	Current Status	Actions to Develop
Key relationship:		
Key relationship:		
Key relationship:		
Key relationship:		
Key relationship:		
Key relationship:		

Making Contact

Once you have determined which relationships to pursue, the next step is to figure out how to gain access to the appropriate people. The following principles embody some proven guidelines:

- *Work locally wherever you employ people.* For legislators and other elected officials, all politics is local. If your company has employees in a given area, the local politicians and those who represent the area in Congress will care about the company that employs them. Get to know the local politicians; they often have connections to state and federal officials. Get to know the legislators representing areas where you employ people. They may not sit on the committees that are most relevant to your activities, but they will know the people who do. "It is important for you to meet with both of your senators and with your local representative," advises one government relations specialist. "Do you have workers who live in other districts, so you could get access to other members? Do you have manufacturing facilities in any other districts? Because you need to get into those."

- *Find out what the decision makers care about.* What issues are important to them? What are their stances on issues you care about? What actions have they taken on issues you care about? "You have to know and understand them," one former government official advises. "Look at their voting records. Get to know them." This kind of thorough knowledge will help you to frame messages that the people you are trying to influence will find persuasive.

- *Get to know the people behind the people.* Part of the job of a congressional staff person is to know about the interests, fears, and problems of the local constituency, and to track the key issues under consideration in the legislature. Take advantage of this. "Congressional staff try faithfully to represent whom they have heard from and sort through the argument on both sides," one Washington insider says. When you talk to staff, you have to be at least as prepared as when you talk to their boss. They are usually on top of the issues. Do not let the apparent youth of some of the aides lead you to underestimate their influence. Staffers at regulatory agencies are likewise a potentially valuable resource. You can have formal input at various points in the regulatory process, but informal discussions with staff members can be very productive. Keep in mind, however, that you should not necessarily be satisfied just to talk to staff members. They may have their own agendas or be unsympathetic to your position. If this is the case, you should probably try to get to the elected official, without antagonizing staffers unnecessarily.

- *Make yourself visible.* You can get to know your representatives in a variety of ways, but you must be proactive about it. Elected officials (and regulators) are open to your opinions, but they will not seek you out, especially if they do not know you. "Just like you market yourself to customers, market yourself to elected officials," says one government relations professional. Make yourself known to them. Attend fundraisers so that you can meet them. Invite local politicians to visit your facility and meet your employees; if the politician you invite can not come, a staff member often will. "Make sure they know how many people you employ," advises one lobbyist, "and make sure he knows the potential impact of the issue on your workers." When you or key people from your organization are next in the Washington area, arrange to meet with legislative and regulatory staff. You might even make a special trip to begin building relationships. Come with a list of issues you want to discuss (though not with specific requests) so that you are not wasting their time. Also offer information they might find useful, as a first step toward establishing a mutually beneficial relationship. If you are knowledgeable about problems that are of concern to other constituents, share your knowledge judiciously.

- *Use the media to leverage yourself.* Businesspeople tend to view media with skepticism, but local (and perhaps regional and national) media can help you build relationships with decision makers. If you develop relationships with members of the press, you can help them meet their need for material while advancing your own interests (Table 4.2). "[Reporters] tend to specialize in things," one regulatory official points out. "So just building a relationship with journalists, being there, giving them ideas about things to write about,

Table 4.2   Building Relationships with the Media

Think about your relationship with the press as symbiotic, not adversarial. Focus on cooperation.

Reporters have to "feed the beast"; they operate according to a daily and weekly news cycle. You can help them by providing information that is newsworthy.

You also can cultivate obligation by providing background briefings on key business issues.

Be proactive and engage reporters. This is the best way to defend against bad publicity.

Match your method to the message. Remember that different forums—press conferences, news releases, and individual interviews—are good for different purposes. Press conferences, for example, are a good way to get information out fast about rapidly emerging issues.

is important." You are not at the mercy of the press. You have something to offer them—access and information. Be prepared to leverage those resources to your advantage. Favorable coverage can influence public opinion about you and the issues you care about. And public opinion in turn influences decision makers in Washington. As one former government official explains, "You can create an awareness of your problem in the press. That may create a more rapid awareness among elected or public officials that there's an issue that needs to be addressed."

Leveraging Internal Resources

Internal resources can help you develop strong relationships with rule makers and referees if you figure out how to organize and leverage them (Table 4.3). Once you decide to make a concerted effort to try to influence governmental decision making, that strategy needs to be disseminated throughout your organization. In other words, you need to prime everyone in your company to play a role in building relationships and influencing government. How do you do that?

Table 4.3 Making the Most of Internal Resources

A large defense contractor periodically counts its employees in different congressional districts. This survey equips the employer to assess the impact of government actions in these districts, and to mobilize employees in several districts and even states to contact policy makers about issues that affect their jobs.

A large manufacturing company brings home the importance of trade relations to its employees by stamping the destination country on each piece of equipment it ships abroad.

An international producer of consumer products has added to its management-evaluation criteria being a good corporate citizen and maintaining relationships with local officials.

A major player in the entertainment industry maintains a database of all its facilities, including who the relevant politicians are, what committees they sit on, and so on.

- *Start at the top.* Senior management has to set a company-wide tone that building relationships with government is important. Many managers, especially in highly regulated industries, view government as the enemy. You not only have to dispel that notion; you also have to encourage the view that government can be influenced in ways that can advance company strategy.

- *Explain to your employees the issues that face your company and point out how they can be influential.* Often politicians are more attentive to appeals from line managers than from senior management. As one former congressman recalls: "I would have lobbyists who would come to me and bring the CEO from the New York office. Well, what did I care what the CEO from the New York office wanted me to do? A good lobbyist would bring the local sales manager for the company in my district. He was far more influential with me than the president of the company." To take advantage of that bias, you can sensitize your managers to understand the importance of being prepared to influence and train them to deal with the media and with politicians. One senior government relations professional surveyed plant managers, asking how many believed that government played a major role in their day-to-day lives. A majority responded that government was fairly irrelevant. Then he asked how much time they devote to adhering to OSHA, EPA, or other regulatory standards and that got them to sit up and take notice. The exercise got across how important government initiatives were in their work lives.

- *Set up communication networks.* Motivating employees calls for keeping them informed about the issues and about what they can do to be heard. Methods for communicating with employees include newsletters, e-mail, and Web pages. Which method you choose will depend on the size and culture of your company, but it is important to establish an effective network of communication. This network will also serve to mobilize employees to act when necessary. According to one former government official who now runs a large corporation, the touchstone to effective employee activity is "not sheer numbers as much as it is the quality of the contact."

Leveraging External Resources

When you are trying to influence government, you need all the support you can get. Other companies in your value net—customers, suppliers, complementors, even competitors—often have a vested interest in the success of your efforts and will often lend support. Leveraging external resources is especially important for small companies with limited internal resources. Like the internal network you build to communicate with and educate your employees, you can set up networks of suppliers, customers, and some complementors and competitors. Once you have these networks in place, you can mobilize the companies in your value net when you need them. "Part of the infrastructure of government relations has to be the plant managers. It has to be the suppliers. It has to be the subcontractors," explains one professional lobbyist. "It is part of the skeleton work that you have to put together if you are going to build some sound government relations."

Another valuable external resource is trade associations. "There is the ability for the trade association to speak quite aggressively, quite dramatically," says one former Washington insider. "They know the politics, they know the people, they know the message-setting role." Even so, you should approach trade associations cautiously and strategically. There are literally thousands of trade associations, and probably hundreds of them are relevant to your business. It is not practical or economical for you to join all of them, so you need to strategically select those with goals most closely aligned with your own. "Check back on previous policy or board decisions. Just to make sure," one lobbyist advises. "It is a lot of work, but if you make a mistake and your opponents are in the same association and they happen to be chairing the committees—then, well, you're toast."

Joining a trade association is likely to present both advantages and disadvantages as summarized in Table 4.4. The value and role of trade associations in your overall influence strategy will depend on such factors as the size of your company, the resources you devote to influence, and whether or not there are trade associations aligned with your interests. Trade associations are particularly useful for small businesses that lack the resources to devote to establishing a Washington office.

Table 4.4 Joining Trade Associations

Advantages	Disadvantages
Offers a well-established and organized mechanism for wielding influence.	All members may not be completely aligned—the association must often cater to the lowest-common-denominator position that members can agree to.
Provides access to decision makers.	
Staff can track progress of legislation and regulation and give you early warning.	You have modest control over decision making and larger members may dominate.
Allows you to have a continuous presence in Washington.	Your specific issues may not be a priority.
	Requires long-term investment of time, money, and resources.

Merely joining a trade association is not enough. To have an impact on its goals, direction, and activities, you have to be an active member: Join committees, attend meetings, get involved in administration of the organization, and the like. "If you really want to move the association on a big issue or have the capacity to move the association on any issue you want," says one former trade-association staff person, "you are well advised to get onto the board—and then to become chairman of a committee, and to use that position."

The CEO of a mid-sized mid-Western oil company, a former Washington insider, has chosen a government relations strategy using only trade associations, his own relationships, and occasional ad hoc coalitions. He has deliberately decided against a Washington office and has operated very successfully. His success is due in large part to the very active role he takes in the associations and on his own. This is not the right strategy for all CEOs, but it certainly works for this company.

The Limits of Relationships

The importance of laying a solid foundation of relationships cannot be overemphasized. But it is equally important to understand what relationships *cannot* do for you:

- *Relationships do not trump deep differences of opinion.* If you take a stance on an issue that is in direct conflict with the political philosophy of key decision makers, do not expect your relationships to carry the day. In the words of one lobbyist, "what they [politicians] are looking for is a balance that is consistent with their political goals and priorities."

- *There are limits to the relationships you can build.* With legislators, you have more leverage in getting access and building relationships because you represent a constituency. With regulators, it is more difficult to build relationships. But personal integrity and a track record as trusted source of information about your industry can help. Regardless, it is important to recognize when you have done all you can, and to know the difference between building relationships and pushing too hard.

- *Access is not influence.* Campaign contributions and fundraisers will gain you access to politicians, but they will not necessarily win you influence. This is a crucial distinction. Your influence will arise from the merits of your arguments, not from the money you contribute. As a former member of Congress explains, "If you have not made a pretty good argument, and spent some time thinking about how you are going to reach this person or thought of a way that's going to help solve some of their problems, you could be in some real trouble."

From Foundations to Strategies

Once you have decided what games you need to play, defined your goals, organized to influence, and begun to build some relationship capital, you are in a strong position to focus on developing influence strategies to achieve specific goals. Part II provides you with approaches to doing that.

PART II

CRAFTING WINNING STRATEGIES

You are now ready to move from building foundations to devising specific operational strategies. Who are you going to try to influence and when? What moves are you going to make and in what order? What messages will you try to convey? Keep in mind that you should not expect to develop a once-and-for-all plan. But you can do your best to look forward, anticipate what opponents will do, and plan out the first few moves.

The next three chapters offer guidance on developing influence strategies. They will show you how to identify leverage points, how to build supportive coalitions, and how to frame persuasive messages. When put together, the resulting action plans will function as the glue that helps to coordinate the many players who are typically involved in influence campaigns. They will also help you, later on, to analyze what worked and what did not; this is essential if you hope to learn all you can from experience.

Identifying Leverage Points: Where Do You Need to Exert Influence?

Pinpointing where and when you need to have an impact essentially means identifying the levels of government at which you will play the game and the key leverage points (processes and decision makers) at each level. Chapter 5 will show you how to do this, providing a framework for understanding government processes and for targeting potential points of leverage.

Building Coalitions: Who Are Your Potential Allies and Adversaries?

You cannot hope to influence rule makers and referees on your own, even if your company is large and powerful, so it is essential to build coalitions. This is why a successful influence strategy calls for identifying others who care about the issue in question. Then you have to figure out how to consolidate your allies and persuade the persuadable. Chapter 6 will show you how to analyze coalitional dynamics and build momentum in favorable directions.

Framing Arguments: What Messages Do You Want to Send?

Once you have pinpointed whom you need to influence and how, you need to figure out how to be influential when you get access. Sound strategy calls for resonant messages—messages that your audience will find influential. This means you need to understand the interests, motivations, and "mental models" of those you seek to influence. Then you have to carefully craft messages that resonate. Chapter 7 will show you how to do that.

As you move on to specific strategies and operational plans, keep in mind that the influence game is highly fluid. Influence plans need to be carefully crafted, but they also need to be flexible, to allow for changes in tactics in response to evolving circumstances. Be prepared to undertake many cycles of learning, planning, testing, and adaptation. As Dwight D. Eisenhower said, "A sound battle plan provides flexibility in both space and time to meet the constantly changing factors. . . . Rigidity inevitably defeats itself." So the goal is not to create a final plan, but to find good starting points and then prepare to be flexible. Put another way, you need to think strategically but act opportunistically.

CHAPTER 5

Identifying Leverage Points

Rule making and refereeing processes are cyclical. During some phases, little or nothing happens; others are a flurry of activity. So you need to figure out when the process is ripe for influence and when such efforts might backfire. "One thing that companies do, which is a big mistake, is coming in with bad timing—way too late, when the decision's already made, or way too early," says a political consultant. "And then they don't get involved later on, when things are really beginning to change. So, unfortunately, one of the things that's necessary is to keep tabs on what's happening."

Shaping government decision making, therefore, calls for knowing where, when, and how to exert influence. But the process of making and enforcing laws is complex in the United States, and its nuances can be difficult to decipher. You have to understand the process if you are to identify the *leverage points* where you can most effectively target your resources. As one former government relations professional put it, "The key to success is to clearly understand the process and how it works. You also need to find out who the key players are and understand as much as possible about them."

In analyzing government processes, some critical things to remember are the following:

- Much of the work of getting legislation passed (or defeated)
  takes place before a bill is even introduced. Later, legislation can die or be changed at many points along the way.

- Laws that affect business are typically implemented by
  regulatory agencies, which write and enforce the rules that
  embody the law. These regulatory processes can also be
  influenced.

- Courts are often used to challenge and enforce laws and
  rules. Court processes are influenced in the usual ways: by
  launching suits and crafting legal arguments.

- The legislative, regulatory, and judicial processes each have
  specific leverage points at which influence is most produc-
  tively directed.

- At each critical leverage point, specific decision makers—
  individuals or groups of people—are pivotal to effective
  influence.

Consider the following examples of how insight into leverage
points yielded advantage in games involving regulatory agencies:

- As mentioned previously, a group of Wall Street rivals
  joined forces in mid-1999 to press for an overhaul of U.S.
  stock markets in response to the advent of electronic exchanges. In a classic example of working with government
  to influence a value-net game, the heads of the dominant
  Wall Street firms met repeatedly with SEC regulators, including one-on-one meetings with Arthur Levitt, Chairman of the SEC. Their efforts appear to have paid off; in
  October 1999, the SEC proposed significant reforms that
  would make it easier for big firms to participate in electronic exchanges. The key to the success of the Wall Street
  alliance was its ability to influence the right regulators at
  the right time.[1]

- In 1997, as privacy advocates increased their pressure on the Federal Trade Commission (FTC) to protect the privacy of Internet users, e-commerce companies were not yet well organized to deal with Washington. Faced with the threat of stiff government regulations, a coalition of Internet service providers and industry advocacy groups created the Online Privacy Alliance for purposes of self-regulation. Led by a former FTC official, the Alliance compiled and promoted a set of self-regulatory standards. This action persuaded the FTC to hold off on new regulations. Three years later, pressure was again being brought, this time in Congress, to pass industry standards. But by this time, the Online Privacy Alliance was in a solid position to influence the agenda and outcome of upcoming legislation.[2]

The Dynamics of Rule Making

The first step in identifying leverage points is to look at rule making, interpretation, and enforcement as a connected system of processes. Decisions made in any arena can be altered elsewhere in the system. Figure 5.1 illustrates the interconnectedness of the three processes and their impact on business.

The overriding point is that the rule making and refereeing processes are intersecting and ongoing. Multiple branches of government often work on the same issues simultaneously, and outside parties always try to influence the outcomes. Thus, you would be well-advised to identify leverage points in each of the major processes: legislative, regulatory, and judicial.

To better understand the nature of this system, we will trace the progress of the Telecommunications Act of 1996. In the process, we will go into some detail about how the legislation was passed, how the Federal Communications Commission (FCC) wrote the rules, and what legal challenges were mounted. The point is not to give a crash course in telecommunications policy. It is to illustrate how a complex, high-stakes piece of legislation got written and interpreted over a period of several years.

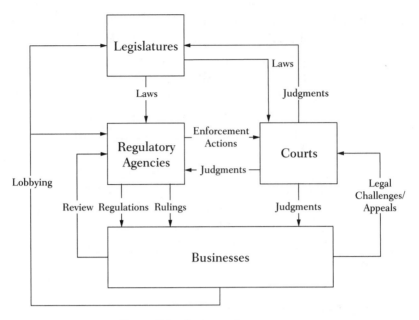

Figure 5.1　Systems of processes.

The Telecommunications Rule Making Game

Prior to the Telecommunications Act of 1996, the principal legislation governing the industry was the Communications Act of 1934. The 1934 Act was essentially a word-for-word amalgamation of sections of the Interstate Commerce Act of the 1880s, which regulated telephones, and the Federal Radio Act of 1927 governing radio. Given the magnitude of post-1934 developments in telecommunications—television, cable, fiber optics, wireless, satellites, and the Internet—it is hardly surprising that pressure for a more fundamental legislative overhaul began building in the 1970s. In 1984, Congress passed the Cable Act, and in 1990 it added amendments dealing with satellites, but the whole structure was noticeably under strain.

The early 1980s also saw the breakup of the Bell monopoly. The result was the creation of AT&T (which served the long-distance market and made equipment) and the Baby Bells, also known as regional Bell operating companies (or RBOCs), which provided local service and were prohibited from manufacturing equipment or offering long-distance or information services. While local telephone service remained a monopoly, the doors were opened to competition in long distance. MCI, Sprint, and a host of smaller companies entered the market. Rules were written governing "access charges," the fees that long-distance companies paid the Baby Bells to connect to local networks. This development led to the advent of companies that circumvented local exchanges by providing large customers direct connections to long-distance switches, further stimulating competition.

By the early 1990s, the Baby Bells—such as Bell Atlantic, Ameritech, and SBC Communications—wanted to get into manufacturing, long distance, and information services, and the long-distance companies wanted access to local customers and sought to overturn the Baby Bells' monopolies (a classic value-net game). At roughly the same time, the FCC was auctioning off spectrum rights for wireless services and both the long-distance companies and the Baby Bells had begun to compete to build mobile networks. The cable companies wanted both deregulation of cable rates and permission to enter the telephone business. Broadcasters were seeking to loosen cross-media ownership restrictions and to prevent the imposition of controls over program content. Internet service providers such as AOL and Compuserve worried that the legislation being contemplated would be the first step toward regulating their industry. Meanwhile, the question of restricting transmission of pornography to minors via the Internet provoked a vigorous debate (a classic public interest game) whose active participants ranged from conservative pro-family organizations to the American Civil Liberties Union.

Thus, the stage was set for a dramatic rule-making contest over the restructuring of an entire industry. In our terms, this was a linked game with value-net and public interest components. Business and nonbusiness players representing a broad spectrum of conflicting interests competed for influence. The telecommunications game involved all three branches of the federal government as well as the states.

The process had three major phases, as we shall see: the drafting and passage of the Act, the writing of rules by the FCC, and the resulting court challenges to the Act and the FCC rules. Recently Congress has stepped in again, to consider legislation that would extend or amend the Act. New legislation will trigger additional rule-writing by the FCC and probably further legal challenges. And so it continues.

Leverage Points in Legislative Processes

In outline form, the Congressional legislative process appears straightforward. (See Figure 5.2 for an overview of the legislative process.) A bill is introduced and referred to a committee, or to multiple committees that consider the bill concurrently, sequentially, or not at all. The bill is then referred to a subcommittee, which will hold hearings on the bill and may schedule a vote. If the bill is voted on favorably, it is sent back to the full committee. If the full committee approves the bill, it is then sent back to the full House (or Senate), which votes on the bill and any amendments that have been attached. The bill is then sent to the other chamber, which follows the same process. If both Houses of Congress pass a bill, it goes to a Conference Committee before proceeding to the president to be signed or vetoed.

In actuality the process has more steps, each of which is permeated with politics, jurisdictional conflicts, and differing priorities. The legislative process can be lengthy and can seem overwhelming, but it has an inherent logic. It also offers multiple leverage points at which the content or direction of a piece of legislation can be influenced. Influencing the process is more complex, of course, than just supporting or opposing laws. Bills are fluid entities. From their origins as mere ideas until they become (or fail to become) laws, bills go through numerous incarnations. Influencing how they are written and amended is as critical as marshalling votes for eventual passage. At each leverage point, an identifiable person or group of people is likely to dominate decision making. It is critical, therefore, to identify the leverage points and the key decision makers at each of those junctures.

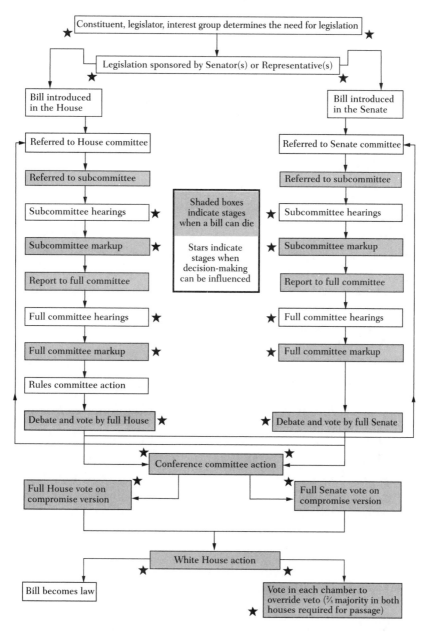

Figure 5.2 How a bill becomes a law: An overview of the legislative process.

Leverage Point 1: Sponsoring and Drafting Legislation

Between 1987 and 1999, an average of 8,915 bills were introduced in each session of Congress, and only 524, or 6 percent, became law.[3] These are encouraging statistics if your goal is to
prevent a law from being passed; if your goal is to create new legislation, you clearly have your work cut out for you.

Proposals for legislation arise from many sources: constituents,
advocacy groups, members of Congress, state and federal agencies,
and the president. Businesses often approach sympathetic members with ideas for legislation. Each bill must have a sponsor within
the House or the Senate, and ultimately both; legislation can be
sponsored by one or more members of Congress. Who sponsors a
bill can have a significant impact on whether it is successful or not.
Members of Congress differ in power and influence, and you
should take that into account if you are looking for a sponsor. Keep
in mind, too, that some members have particular areas of expertise
in which they command respect from their colleagues.

To find the right sponsors for your initiatives, try first to find a
legislator on a key committee who will take up your cause. "You
need to find your champion, someone who can help you get co-
sponsors," explains one former staffer. "You'd want to get that
champion to write a 'Dear colleague' letter to the members of the
committee saying, 'This is great stuff, and I think you should sign
on to it.' If you're lucky, you'll get every member of that committee
to sign on. So you do that, and you work toward resolving, damp-
ening, removing any kind of obstacles or persons who you'd think
might be obstructionists." Often, the committee staff is the best
place to start to find a potential sponsor. Committee staffers are
specialists; members turn to them for advice on particular issue
areas, and they usually draft the legislation.

The bill that eventually became the Telecommunications Act
was introduced in the Senate in March 1995 by Senator Larry
Pressler (R-SD), Chairman of the Senate Commerce Committee.
Shortly after the Senate passed it, the House began considera-
tion of a companion bill introduced by Thomas Bliley (R-VA),
Chairman of the House Commerce Committee. Pressler, known

to be a supporter of the Bell companies, was pressing for a so-called "date certain" when long-distance service would be opened up to Baby Bells. Bliley leaned more toward the long-distance companies, and his bill reflected that: It called for market tests to guarantee that a certain degree of competition existed in local markets before the Baby Bells would be permitted to provide long-distance services. One observer speculated about some of the reasons for Bliley's position: "AT&T has always had a presence in the Richmond area. They were a large local employer. They were a constituent."

Leverage Point 2: Referral to Committee

After being introduced and assigned a number, bills are sent or referred to the appropriate committee. There are 18 standing (permanent) committees in the House and 17 in the Senate, as well as three joint committees that have oversight responsibilities but no legislative authority. Committees range from 10 to 60 members, and the chair and a majority of the members represent the majority party.

The committee a bill is referred to can have a significant impact on its viability. So you should figure out which committees and subcommittees will be most sympathetic to your cause. Different committees are likely to respond differently to the same piece of legislation, which should be taken into consideration in the drafting stage: A measure may be written in such a way that it will be referred to a committee likely to report on it favorably. One way to ensure that a given piece of legislation is referred to a specific committee is to write it as an amendment to a bill that is ahead of it in the pipeline; amendments are always referred to the committee that considered the original measure.

Committee referrals are usually routine, but there are occasional disagreements over jurisdiction. The Speaker of the House has control over the referral process in that body; in the Senate, the presiding officer[4] makes referrals, but they are subject to appeals from the floor. The Senate version of the Telecommunications bill was referred to the Commerce Committee. In the House, the bill went to both the Commerce Committee and the Judiciary Committee, the latter because the AT&T consent decree had been under the aegis of the Justice Department. The result was some tension between the committees. "A lot of what goes on in Congress concerns jurisdictional turf," says one long-term observer. "Committees are very jealous of their power. On one hand, you have communications policy supposedly being made in the Commerce Committee. On the other hand, the consent decree was the purview of Judiciary. So there were some interesting coalitions that cut across committee boundaries." Ultimately, the House Judiciary Committee did not take up the bill.

Leverage Point 3: Committee Work

Most of the real substantive work of the legislative process is done within committees and subcommittees. Each senator and representative serves on several committees and subcommittees, which means that at any given time he or she is dealing with dozens of pieces of legislation. (For a list of the main committees and subcommittees that deal with business issues, see Table 5.1.)

Committee work is arguably the most important leverage point in the legislative process. Of the several thousand bills referred to committees during each session of Congress, only a small number are chosen by committee chairs for consideration. The committee chair refers those that are selected to the appropriate subcommittee; each committee has several subcommittees, with anywhere from 4 to over 30 members apiece. The House version of the Telecommunications Act was referred to the Telecommunications, Trade and Consumer Protection Subcommittee.

Because committee and subcommittee chairs wield substantial power, it is essential that you cultivate those who are sympathetic to your position. Selected by the majority party, usually on the basis of seniority, committee chairs have broad discretionary powers: control of the committee's agenda, referrals to subcommittees, and management of committee funds and committee staff. Subcommittee chairs likewise control their own agendas, timetables, and witness lists. The chair can create an atmosphere

Table 5.1   Key Congressional Committees and Subcommittees

House	Senate
Standing Committees (Number of Members)	
Agriculture (51)	Agriculture, Nutrition, and Forestry (18)
Appropriations (61)	Appropriations (28)
Armed Services (60)	Armed Services (20)
Banking and Financial Services (60)	Banking, Housing, and Urban Affairs (20)
Budget (24)	Budget (22)
Commerce (53)	Commerce, Science, and Transportation (20)
Education and the Workforce (49)	Energy and Natural Resources (20)
Government Reform (44)	Environment and Public Works (18)
House Administration (9)	Finance (20)
International Relations (49)	Foreign Relations (18)
Judiciary (37)	Governmental Affairs (16)
Resources (50)	Judiciary (18)
Rules (13)	Health, Education, Labor and Pensions (18)
Science (47)	Rules and Administration (16)
Small Business (35)	Small Business (18)
Standards of Official Conduct (10)	Veterans' Affairs (12)
Transportation and Infrastructure (64)	Indian Affairs (14)
Veterans' Affairs (31)	
Ways and Means (38)	

Joint Committees

Joint Committee on Taxation (10)
Joint Economic Committee (20)
Joint Committee on the Library of Congress (10)

Subcommittees of a Few Major Committees (Number of Members)

Commerce Committee:

- Telecommunications, Trade and Consumer Protection (29)
- Finance and Hazardous Materials (29)
- Health and Environment (31)
- Energy and Power (31)
- Oversight and Investigations (19)

Commerce, Science, and Transportation Committee:

- Aviation (18)
- Communications (17)
- Consumer Affairs, Foreign Commerce and Tourism (7)
- Manufacturing and Competitiveness (9)
- Oceans and Fisheries (7)
- Science, Technology and Space (9)
- Surface Transportation and Merchant Marine (14)

(continued)

Table 5.1 Continued

House	Senate
Judiciary Committee:	Finance Committee:
• Commercial and Administrative Law (10)	• Health Care (14)
	• International Trade (16)
• The Constitution (13)	• Long-Term Growth and Debt Reduction (4)
• Courts and Intellectual Property (16)	
• Crime (13)	• Social Security and Family Policy (10)
• Immigration and Claims (13)	• Taxation and IRS Oversight (11)
Banking and Financial Services Committee:	Banking, Housing, and Urban Affairs Committee:
• Housing and Community Opportunity (26)	• Securities (16)
	• Financial Institutions (16)1
• Financial Institutions and Consumer Credit (28)	• International Trade and Finance (9)
	• Housing and Transportation (9)
• Domestic and International Monetary Policy (26)	• Economic Policy (7)
• Capital Markets, Securities, and Government-Sponsored Enterprises (28)	
• General Oversight and Investigations (10)	

of opposition or support for a bill within the committee; the chair can also control whether a bill gets on the agenda for consideration and the pace at which it is dealt with. Because committees typically deal with many pieces of legislation simultaneously, only a few of which can proceed to the floor, death through delay is commonplace. On the other hand, a strong coalition within a committee can move a bill along.

Bills with vigorous support can be pushed through quickly while those with strong opposition often get bogged down in procedural problems. The chair can also stack the witness list, or limit the number of witnesses or the duration of their testimony. So working with the committee chairman to influence him to speed along or delay consideration of a bill is a potent way to exert influence.

Both committee staffs and the staffs of individual members are influential in the legislative process. Legislation is typically researched and drafted by staff members, who work very closely with committee members and therefore have a great deal of influence on members' opinions. To influence the content of legislation, it is worthwhile to work hard to sway committee staff while a bill is still in the formative stages.

The coalitions that developed in key committees over the Telecommunication Act crossed party lines in interesting ways. While Senator Pressler, the Republican, was sympathetic to the Baby Bells and supported a "date certain," Senator Ernest Hollings (D-SC) was widely known to distrust the Bells and wanted a market test. In the House, the party affiliations were reversed: John Dingell (D-MI), who had ties to Ameritech and the Communications Workers of America, was pushing for the date certain, while the Republican, Chairman Bliley, supported the market test. This was clearly not an issue that fell along clear party lines.

The sympathies of the key decision makers are, unsurprisingly, reflected in business contributions to their campaigns. Sympathies typically drive contributions, not the reverse. During the 1996 election cycle, AT&T was the third largest contributor to Chairman Bliley, donating $10,000 to his campaign. GTE, the National Association of Broadcasters, and General Electric (parent of NBC) were also top-20 contributors, donating $6,500, $6,000, and $5,250 respectively. The picture for Representative Dingell was quite different. His top-20 contributors included Bell South ($20,500), U.S. West ($11,743), the National Cable Television Association ($10,000), the National Association of Broadcasters ($10,000), and Ameritech ($9,000). Senator Hollings' top-20 contributors over the 1993–1998 period included Time Warner (number 5), AT&T (7), Sprint (8), Bell Atlantic (9), MCI WorldCom (10), Tele-Communications Inc. (11), News Corporation (12), CBS (13), and the National Association of Broadcasters (17). Meanwhile, some members were more focused on getting the right technical solution than on the politics. Senator John McCain (R-AZ) opposed all of the existing proposals. McCain argued that companies should not be subsidized and that low-income people should get subsidies instead. But his proposed amendment never got out of the Committee.

Leverage Point 4: Hearings and Mark-Up

When a bill reaches a subcommittee's agenda, the subcommittee studies it, asks executive branch agencies for written comments, compiles a witness list, and sends out invitations to testify at hearings. Witnesses submit preliminary written testimony and then deliver a prepared statement and answer questions from members of the Committee. Following hearings, the bill may be allowed to die or the subcommittee may hold a mark-up session at which the bill is debated and amendments are proposed. If a majority of subcommittee members support it, the bill goes back to the full committee for possible further hearings or revisions.

Hearings and mark-up sessions both represent opportunities to influence the eventual vote and hence are key leverage points. Within a committee, those in the majority on specific issues often push for witnesses who will endorse their position and provide political and public support for it, while opponents seek witnesses who will agree with them. This is an important leverage point: influencing who is invited to testify can help shape the public record and persuade undecided subcommittee members to support your position.

Mark-up sessions also offer opportunities to delay the process. A committee member who opposes a bill can propose numerous amendments to make the bill more or less palatable and therefore less likely to pass. Mark-up strategies differ in the House and the Senate due to the relative sizes of the committees. Coalitions are more important in the House, where committees are much larger. In the case of the Telecommunications Act, the opposing long distance and Baby Bell camps were actively involved in the mark-up process. "For the purposes of lobbying, the Bells can do things they could never do in business—they'd get thrown in jail," one observer commented. "So they first met weekly and then daily in drafting sessions on the versions of the bills they wanted, and they were working through staff that supported their position."

Once a committee has completed and debated the bill, it votes and reports its vote to the main chamber. If a committee does not support a bill, it usually takes no action other than voting it down. It is rare for a bill to be reported without amendments. Sometimes a committee recommends that a bill that is extensively amended be redrafted as a *clean bill.*

After two days of hearings and one day of mark-up, the House subcommittee forwarded the amended version of the Telecommunications Act to the full committee for consideration. After its own mark-up session, the full Commerce Committee approved the amended bill. The legislation that left the committee largely favored the interests of long-distance companies and left the Baby Bells somewhat in the lurch.

Leverage Point 5: Floor Action

In the Senate, a bill that is reported out of committee goes to the full Senate for floor action. In the House most bills go first to the Rules Committee, which sets parameters and time limits for debate and amendment, including specification of further amendments that can be considered on the House floor. Since the Speaker of the House handpicks most members of the Rules Committee, he retains substantial control over its decisions. The Rules Committee's power resides in its control of scheduling and its ability to allow or prohibit further amendments. It expedites high-priority measures, protects partisan agendas, and creates an orderly process for floor action on important bills.

Once a bill reaches the floor, it is debated, amended, and voted on. Floor amendments can drastically change the content of a bill, leaving it very different than when it arrived. This phase offers new opportunities for you to modify the legislation or simply effect delay. If you have been unsuccessful in earlier attempts to shape the legislation, this is an opportunity to try again, in a setting in which all the members of the House or Senate, not just committee members, can decide on the fate of the legislation. This is a particularly critical point if your "champion" is not a member of the committee to which the bill was referred.

The broadcast industry and its allies successfully used floor action to advance their position in the Senate debate. The Senate passed amendments to the telecommunications bill that would immediately deregulate cable rates and eliminate restrictions on how many television and radio stations a single company could own—both big victories for the broadcast industry. The Senate also handed broadcasters some setbacks, approving amendments that (1) provided for full scrambling of sexually explicit adult programming, (2) required broadcasters to solicit viewer input on the violent content of programming prior to license renewal, (3) required mechanisms for limiting the exposure of children to violent television programming, (4) discouraged access by children to obscene and indecent material through the Internet, and (5) expressed "the sense of the Senate" that violent and aggressive programming on television should be limited.

The vote in the Senate did not split along party lines and revealed some interesting coalitions. Senator Dole supported McCain's amendment, annoying the Bells, even though he was already planning to seek his party's presidential nomination later in the year. Then there was the "farm team," a bipartisan group of senators (including Senator Pressler from South Dakota) whose farm states have a lot of small rural phone companies. They introduced language into the statute to the effect that, notwithstanding the virtues of competition and lowering entry barriers, state regulatory commissions did not have to permit the entry of new players into rural areas if they believed the resulting system would not be sustainable. These small companies were cash cows, because they received a lot of money in interconnection fees from the big companies.

In the House, a surprising last minute turn-around occurred when the Republican leadership, led by Speaker Newt Gingrich, ordered a rewrite favorable to the Baby Bells and thus lost the support of the long-distance companies and the Democrats, who largely favored strong restrictions on the Baby Bells. The new version reduced the number of hurdles the Baby Bells had to pass in order to enter the long-distance market.

Another contentious issue was media ownership. The existing rules prohibited any one company from owning television stations that reached more than 25 percent of the nation's households. A proposed amendment to raise that limit to 50 percent brought an immediate threat of a presidential veto.

A third issue was controlling violent and sexually explicit programming on television in order to protect children. First Amendment advocates were alarmed that any controls would be akin to censorship; others believed that the broadcast industry should be compelled to take some responsibility for the content of programming.

Meanwhile, the cable companies wanted to see rates deregulated and to be allowed to enter the telephone business. The Baby Bells wanted to get into the video business. All the telephone companies wanted an end to restrictions on their ability to buy cable companies. So a compromise emerged.

In the end, compromises were reached on all three issues, moving the House version closer to the Senate version. Key amendments allowed the Baby Bells to offer long-distance services after meeting certain minimum requirements, limited single-company ownership of television stations to 35 percent of all viewers, and required manufacturers of televisions to install the V-chip. There were no clear winners in either the House or the Senate version, but the Baby Bells fared better in the House, mostly due to Gingrich's influence.

Table 5.2 summarizes the differences between the House and Senate bills. The whole package then headed to the Conference Committee, where the differences between the two versions would be hammered out.

Leverage Point 6: Conference Committee

Once both chambers have passed similar measures, the two bills go to a conference committee—a temporary body composed of members from both chambers, created specifically for a given piece of legislation. The job of the committee is to work out a compromise version of the bill, which is then sent to each chamber for

Table 5.2   Comparison of the House and Senate Telecommunications Bills

House	Senate
Cable Television	
• Immediately deregulates rates of small cable systems	• Immediately deregulates rates of small cable systems
• **Deregulates rates of other systems in 15 months**	• **Deregulates rates of companies that do not exceed the national average**
Broadcast Television/Radio	
• Allows one company to own an unlimited number of television stations nationally, covering up to 35 percent of viewers	• Allows one company to own an unlimited number of television stations nationally, covering up to 35 percent of viewers
• Allows one company to own an unlimited number of radio stations	• Allows one company to own an unlimited number of radio stations
• **Retains prohibition on a single company owning both a television station and a cable system in the same locale**	• **Lifts laws barring a single company from owning both a television station and a cable system in the same locale**
• **Lifts local-ownership restrictions to allow a single company to own multiple media outlets (newspaper, television, and radio)**	• **No provisions about local ownership of multiple media outlets**
Local Phone Service	
• Preempts state barriers to permit cable companies and long-distance companies to provide local phone service	• Preempts state barriers to permit cable companies and long-distance companies to provide local phone service
Long Distance	
• Removes consent decree that broke up AT&T	• Removes consent decree that broke up AT&T
• **Forbids Bells from providing long-distance service until its long-distance competitor provides local phone service**	• **No provision regarding Bells**
Television Sex and Violence	
• Requires television-set makers to install a V-chip in new sets enabling purchasers to block shows	• Requires television-set makers to install a V-chip in new sets enabling purchasers to block shows

Key differences are in boldface.

a final "up or down" vote. The conferees (also known as managers) are appointed by the Speaker and the Senate presiding officer, who can influence the process by selecting conferees who will advance a specific agenda. Conferees are usually members of the committees that originally reported on the bill, but there is no requirement that each chamber appoint the same number of conferees; because conferees from each chamber vote as a delegation, relative numbers make no difference.

A conference committee is another key leverage point. Its overriding goal is to hammer out a compromise version of the bill that will be acceptable to majorities in both chambers and to the White House. So your ability to influence the Administration's position can have a powerful impact here. Also, legislators often prime bills for conference by deliberately adding or omitting provisions as bargaining chips. Among the few formal rules governing a conference committee's proceedings is a requirement that it meet at least once in open session, and public scrutiny adds an extra layer of complexity to the bargaining process. Lobbying of conferees is intense.

The only hope for those who wanted the telecommunications bill enacted, given the president's veto threats and the differences between the two versions, was compromise in the conference committee. The process was contentious and riddled with delays. Each chamber had its own priorities, and compromises had to be negotiated with the White House. The most bitterly fought issues were media concentration and the rules governing local phone companies' entry into the long-distance market. Alarmed that the restrictions on the Baby Bells were too lax, a group of senators made a failed last-minute attempt to reintroduce an oversight role for the Justice Department.

After months of negotiation, a joint version of the bill was agreed to. It passed both houses the next day. One regulator who observed the lobbying efforts of the Baby Bells and the long-distance companies commented, "In the end they sort of neutralized each other, and we ended up with something that was an imperfect but reasonable balance." Another recalled, "It was a model of ambiguity. . . . There was one senator who knew there were going to be problems after the thing was signed, because he got a call from the CEO of AT&T saying, 'Senator, you're a great American, this is a wonderful piece of legislation. Congratulations!' He barely had hung up the phone and he got a call from the CEO of a Bell company saying, 'Senator, you're a great American. . . .'"

Leverage Point 7: Presidential Action

When both Houses of Congress have passed identical versions of a bill, it goes to the president to be signed or vetoed. If the president takes no action within 10 days, the bill automatically becomes law. (If Congress is about to adjourn, the president can refuse to act before the adjournment and the bill dies; this is known as a "pocket veto.") If the president vetoes a bill, two-thirds of both houses must vote to override the veto.[5]

The arrival of a bill on the president's desk is by no means the first moment when the executive branch can influence the legislative process. You should factor in the impact of Administration action from the beginning and work to build support within the relevant agencies. The president can propose legislation—a member of Congress must introduce it—and he can pressure members of Congress as the leader of his party and through his control over party campaign funds that affect members' districts.

The president uses the State of the Union address and economic and budget reports to communicate his priorities to Congress, and he has constant access to the media to promote his Administration's agendas and policies. The White House and administrative agencies have congressional liaisons who keep close track of legislative activity. Finally, the threat of a presidential veto can be used to influence how legislation gets written and amended. When members vote on important legislation, they can generally count on receiving a message from the White House, making clear the president's position.

The compromise telecommunications bill almost fell apart at the last minute when Vice President Gore prematurely announced a victory for the Administration on national television. Republican leaders reasoned that if Gore was so happy, they must have given away too much. Ruffled feathers were smoothed, and President Clinton signed the Act into law on February 8, 1996, ending the battle in one forum and shifting it to the next one: the writing of rules by the Federal Communications Commission.

Leverage Point 8: Authorizations and Appropriations

The budget process accounts for a very high proportion of congressional activity. The core of the budget process—an annual exercise that begins in February and continues through September—is a pair of activities that go hand-in-hand: authorizations and appropriations. First Congress must pass legislation authorizing each federal agency and program, both new and continuing. Each authorization must be approved by both houses and signed by the president for a program or agency to begin or continue operations.

Before any money can be allocated to an activity, however, a separate appropriations bill must also pass through the process. Authorization does not guarantee appropriation. This two-step process often creates tensions between the authorizing and appropriating committees. Authorizers may want more money than appropriators are willing to give, or appropriators may approve spending "pending" later authorization. If an authorizing committee cannot get its bills approved, its chairman will sometimes simply ask the chairman of the appropriations committee to provide the money anyway; this often happens with foreign aid bills.

This dual process is critical to understand. You can invest enormous resources getting legislation passed only to find its appropriations blocked. The appropriations process, and the key decision makers within it, thus merit close attention. Viewed from the opposite angle, the appropriations process is a key defensive leverage point: If you failed to block legislation that you oppose, you can still achieve your goals by blocking the appropriations.

Outcomes

Legislation to reform the telecommunications industry was signed into law by President Clinton in February 1996. The

Telecommunications Act of 1996 represented the most sweeping set of changes to the industry in 60 years:

- *Telephone.* Baby Bells were permitted to provide long-distance service outside their regions immediately and inside their regions once they eliminated entry barriers to competition for local service. Long-distance carriers could enter local markets, but were restricted in their ability to market local and long-distance services as a package.

- *Cable television.* Rates for all cable services except "basic" were no longer regulated. Telephone companies were permitted to offer cable services. Cable systems were required to scramble sexually explicit programming.

- *Radio and television broadcasting.* Media-concentration rules were relaxed, allowing any single company or network to own television stations that reached as many as 35 percent of all U.S. households (up from 25 percent). Networks were allowed to own cable systems but not other networks. Nationwide limits on radio-station ownership were repealed. All new televisions were required to contain the V-chip, to enable parents to control the programming their children watch.

- *Internet and online services.* The Communications Decency (CDA) portion of the Act imposed criminal penalties for transmission over the Internet of material considered "indecent to minors." It also criminalized transmissions intended to annoy or harass. Online services with voluntary blocking software were protected from prosecution. (*Note:* In response to a challenge by the American Civil Liberties Union, the Supreme Court later struck down the CDA as an unconstitutional violation of First Amendment rights.)

All sides tried to claim victory, but some clearly fared better than others; most would have to await the drafting of regulations by the FCC to assess the full implications of the legislation. As one analyst described it, "Arrived at through the course of intense Congressional lobbying, the law that was eventually adopted represented a carefully crafted compromise rather than a bold blueprint for the future."[6] The final provisions left the Baby Bells complaining about the restrictions on their entry into the long-distance market, and the long-distance companies scrambling to figure out how to deal with their impending competition. The cable-television and broadcast industries suddenly had lots of scope for expansion. Online providers were dealt heavy penalties for transmission of indecent material, but they later prevailed in court. In the end, every participant got some items on its wish list but no one was completely satisfied.

Leverage Points in Rule-Writing Processes

Congress ordinarily passes laws that communicate the intent of a policy but do not spell out how it is to be implemented. Instead, the appropriate federal agencies interpret the intent of the law and write the rules and regulations that will embody it. The rules issued by departments, agencies, and commissions are law; they carry the same weight as congressional legislation, presidential executive orders, and judicial decisions.[7] The regulatory process often has a more direct impact than the legislative process on the bottom line of many businesses, but it is far less well understood. (For a list of the major federal regulatory agencies with an impact on business, see Table 5.3.) There are literally hundreds of other agencies at the federal level alone. By and large, the basic elements of the rule-making process are similar from one agency to another and from one issue to another.

The regulatory process typically consists of distinct phases, beginning when the law is passed and ending when the rules are published. Much of the regulatory process is codified—that is, agencies must follow specific procedural rules governing such matters as the number of days allowed for responses and who has the right to be heard. (For an overview of the phases of a typical rule-writing process, see Table 5.4.) Sometimes these rules are challenged, prolonging the process. The critical phases in the rule-making process address gathering technical input, defining how the rules will be written, drafting and editing, getting feedback both internally and externally, and approving the final rule.

Table 5.3   Major Regulatory Agencies Whose Rule Making Impacts Business

The Environmental Protection Agency (EPA). An independent agency whose mission is to protect human health and safeguard the natural environment. It regulates air and water pollution, which includes setting emissions and energy-efficiency standards. EPA regulations can seriously affect manufacturing, transportation, and utility industries.

The Federal Aviation Administration (FAA). An agency of the Department of Transportation. Its main responsibilities are regulating air commerce, developing civil aviation and airports, managing airspace, and regulating air traffic.

The Federal Communications Commission (FCC). An independent agency charged with regulating interstate and international communications by radio, television, wire, satellite, and cable. Its seven bureaus are responsible for developing and implementing regulations, issuing licenses, and investigating complaints and violations.

The Food and Drug Administration (FDA). An agency of the Department of Health and Human Services whose mission is to ensure that foods are pure and produced under sanitary conditions, that drugs and medical devices are safe, that cosmetics are safe, and that labels and packaging on all such products are accurate.

The Federal Trade Commission (FTC). An independent agency that enforces antitrust laws and ensures consumer protection. Anticompetitive behavior, predatory behavior, and unfair or deceptive market practices fall under its purview.

The Occupational Safety and Health Administration (OSHA). An agency of the Department of Labor, provides for occupational safety by reducing hazards in the workplace and enforcing job-safety standards. OSHA regulations apply to most private businesses in the United States.

Because the regulatory process almost always adheres to the prescribed sequence, the leverage points at which the process can be influenced are predictable. Certain points in this process offer opportunities to be influential—sometimes officially and sometimes unofficially. The key is to recognize these points and to build your reputation with the individuals who are instrumental at each. "The process of getting yourself known is something that doesn't happen overnight, and it takes a concerted strategic effort by someone on the appropriate level of the company's staff to approach someone on the commensurate level in the agency," a former regulator advises. "It could be a technical staff person to a technical staff person. In fact, that's sometimes the best way, because that technical person in the agency then can begin to turn

Table 5.4 Leverage Points

Phase 1: Analysis of Legislation
What the law says
Defines
- Purpose of rule making
- Schedule
- Which agency has jurisdiction?
- Level of agency control and responsibility

Phase 2: Where the Ideas Come From
What the rules should say
Legislated content
- Deadlines
- Default provisions
Internal agency input
- Senior agency staff
- Advisory committees
- Program office
- General counsel
- Field and enforcement staff
External input
- White House
- Congress
- Other agencies
- **Interest groups**
- **Businesses**
- Interested individuals

Phase 3: Authorization
Preparing to write the rules
- Set agency priorities
- Allocate staff resources

Phase 4: Planning
How the rules will be written/who will write them
- Identify goals
- Establish legal requirements
- Establish information requirements
- Develop plan for participation
Written comments or public hearing?
Whom to invite?

Phase 5: Drafting Rules
Writing/editing the rules
- Data collection and analysis
- Impact studies
  —How will small business be affected?
  —How much paperwork is required?
  —What are the environmental impacts?
- Internal discussions
- **External discussions (unofficial)**
- Draft rules and implementation plan

Phase 6: Internal Review
Getting informal feedback within the agency
Solicit peer feedback
- Program offices
- Policy analysts
- Research and development
- Field/enforcement staff
- Advisory groups
Solicit supervisory feedback
- General counsel
- Senior agency management
- **Political leaders**

Phase 7: External Review
Getting informal feedback from outside the agency
- Office of Management and Budget
- Congress
- **Interest groups**
- **Affected businesses**
- Other agencies

Phase 8: Public Input
Official processes for soliciting feedback
- **Publish notice of process in *Federal Register***
- **Review written comments**
- **Hold hearings**
- Review and analyze input
- Respond to public input

Phase 9: Approvals—Possible Actions (Next Steps)
Internal agency decision making on final rules
1. Approve rule with no changes (Publish in *Federal Register*)
2. Approve rule with minor changes (Repeat phases 6 and 7)
3. Need another round of public input (Repeat phase 8)
4. Make major change to rule (Return to phase 5)
5. Abandon current rule and start over (Return to phase 3)
6. Decide there is no need for rule (Publish in *Federal Register*)

Phase 10: Epilogue
It is never over
Rules can be challenged by
- Staff interpretations
- Technical variations
- **Petitions for reconsideration**
- **Litigation**

Boldface indicates leverage points.

to the technical staff person in the company for questions—for kind of a sounding-board, idea testing."

The official process offers opportunities to submit written feedback on proposed rules and to testify at hearings. In these forums, you will almost certainly encounter others who are also trying to influence the process. Unofficially, the process offers multiple opportunities for input before the rules are written and while they are being edited. Access to these unofficial opportunities depends on having established relationships with the pertinent agency staff. "There are instances where, before a set of rules are published, the agency typically is involved in informal and sometimes formal discussions with the stakeholders," explains one former regulatory official. "And the people who are likely to be invited to talk with the agency prior to the rules being proposed are the people that the staff know."

Keep in mind that regulators have different motivations than legislators. Their focus is more technical and less political. Regulators, after all, are not elected. The regulatory process is also more structured than the legislative process; it is far from simple, but it is orderly. Thus, once you understand the process and establish relationships within it, you can manage it. Recall the efforts of the fiber-optic firm Global Crossing, discussed in Chapter 2: By carefully building relationships and applying pressure in the right places, Global Crossing delayed the competition long enough to get its own system in place.

Finally, self-regulation and negotiated rule making are often attractive alternatives to conventional rule making processes. You should evaluate early on whether you think your interests would be better served by trying to preempt regulation with your own proposals or to enter into negotiations with regulatory agencies.

Writing the Rules

After it was signed into law, the Telecommunications Act of 1996 was subject to an extensive interpretation and rule making process within the Federal Communications Commission (FCC), the regulatory agency responsible for its implementation. Here again, key players sought to influence the process by direct and indirect means.

Each of the FCC's bureaus (see Table 5.5) initiates rule making for its area of jurisdiction; the provisions of this legislation were so sweeping that the bureaus that regulate cable services, common carriers (telephone and telegraph), and mass media (radio and television) all became involved. Each bureau further subdivided the legislation into its components, and each component proceeded separately through the phases of rule making. It is a painstaking and arduous process to ensure that rules are written to cover every foreseeable contingency.

The Act required the FCC to write 80 new rules covering a dizzying array of issues. Many had to be written within six months, the rest within 18 months. In opening up local phone markets, for example, the FCC had to determine how new providers would connect to established phone networks to enable customers of new companies to call customers of old companies and vice-versa. Other rules covered how to break down local networks into leasable components so that long-distance companies could lease network capacity, and how to determine when Baby

Table 5.5 Major Bureaus of the FCC

Cable Services Bureau. Implements and enforces the Cable Television Consumer Protection and Competition Act of 1992.

Common Carrier Bureau. Regulates telephone and telegraph.

International Bureau. Handles all FCC international telecommunications and satellite programs and policies.

Mass Media Bureau. Regulates AM, FM, and television broadcast stations and related facilities.

Wireless Telecommunication Bureau. Regulates wireless companies serving the communications needs of businesses, individuals, nonprofit organizations, and state and local governments.

Enforcement Bureau (established in 1997 after the Act). Enforces the Telecommunications Act, as well as Commission rules, orders, and authorization.

Bells had allowed enough local competition to earn entry into the long-distance market.

Congress's directions to the FCC led to problems. "Because they knew it was going to be really hard, Congress said, 'Do local competition rules in six months, and then within a year do universal service reform,'" one observer explained. "They never mentioned access reform at all, but it was implicit, so it had to be done. But they got the sequencing backward. So the FCC developed a 14-point checklist for local competition before they got to price reform."

The scope of the legislation and the short time frame led to a frenzied process. The FCC's then-Chairman Reed Hundt likened the challenge to Lewis and Clark's expedition into uncharted territory. In an effort to solicit input efficiently, the FCC solicited opinions early on from members of trade associations and consumer groups, and was inundated with requests to meet with business executives. Several large pending mergers (AT&T and TCI, Ameritech and SBC) also were working their way through the FCC approval process. The White House pressured the FCC to hold off decisions on the mergers while Congress weighed in on how the rules should be written for the regional Bell companies.

The FCC used an accelerated process—getting input, drafting proposed rules, soliciting feedback, and writing final rules. The process was more analytical than many regulatory processes. "Traditionally there had been a lot of lobbying," explains one regulator. "A commissioner might ask his staff, 'who's in favor, who's opposed, and who will be upset if we do X, Y, or Z?' Hundt was asking different questions: 'Where's the analysis? What are the incentives? What has to be done to ensure competition takes hold?' By the time the Act passed, the companies had figured this out. They ended up hiring economists, running models, and presenting numbers. AT&T and some of the smaller long-distance companies did excellent analyses and presented better theories of forward-looking costs versus historical cost. The cable companies also hired first-rate telecom economists."

The lesson is that you have to adapt your influence strategies to the demands of the situation. In this rule making process, data, analysis, and presentation of results were decisively important. The best players recognized this and adjusted accordingly.

At the six-month deadline, the agency issued rules that primarily addressed telephone issues, hoping to strike a balance among competing phone-company interests. The new rules, which adhered to the middle of the road, had the following key components:

- Local phone companies must allow new competitors—including long-distance, cable, and wireless firms—to plug into their networks.

- Baby Bells must offer discounts of 17 to 25 percent to competitors who buy their phone service in bulk for resale, plus low prices for separate parts of their local networks.

- Fees that wireless phone companies pay to complete calls on the wired phone network will be cut drastically, eventually leading to lower cellular-phone rates to consumers.

- As the Baby Bells allow competition in local markets, they will be allowed to compete in the long-distance market.

No one was entirely happy with the final rules, but the Baby Bells were the big losers. Not only did they have to open up their local phone markets to competition; they also had to wait to enter the long-distance market until they had met stringent criteria.

Leverage Points in Judicial and Regulatory Refereeing Processes

The courts are routinely called on to interpret the validity of new laws and to intercede if a regulatory agency has exceeded its legislative authority. (For an overview of the federal judicial system, see Figure 5.3.) Courts are also forums for disputes over the application of existing law. The structure of the court system allows for these disputes to be played out at different levels, and offers several opportunities to appeal unfavorable decisions. For example, a

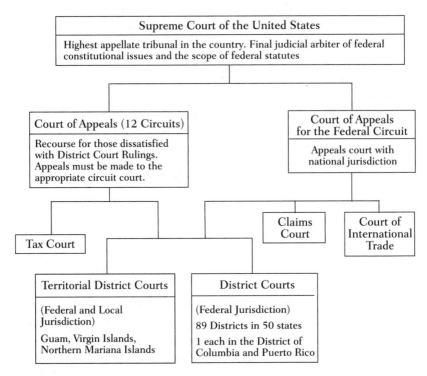

Figure 5.3   Federal court system of the United States. The federal court system resembles a pyramid, with the Supreme Court at the apex, the appeals courts below it and the district courts at the base. Most cases that require federal attention begin at the district-court level. If a party is dissatisfied with the ruling of a district court, the first course of action is to file an appeal with the appeals court. In general, the Supreme Court only hears cases with constitutional ramifications. Each state has its own court system as well. The Constitution specifies matters over which the federal courts have authority; almost everything else is handled at the state level. A suit involving a federal agency or employee would be handled at the federal level, for example; a case involving a state agency would be dealt with in the state courts. The lines of demarcation get fuzzy when a case involves businesses that operate in multiple states or a dispute between states.

decision in federal district court that the Communications Decency part of the Telecommunications Act was unconstitutional was appealed by the Justice Department (at the urging of its sponsors in Congress) to the Supreme Court.

The pros and cons of pursuing a dispute through the judicial system should be weighed very carefully. The judicial system is less susceptible to influence than the legislative or regulatory processes; once an issue has entered the court system, your ability to influence the process is restricted to making persuasive legal arguments. A positive outcome in the courts can have an impact in the legislative and regulatory arenas—but so can a negative outcome.

Court cases can also be very costly for your company, and not just in financial terms. Think of the precious management time that has been lost to Microsoft as a result of its antitrust case. Even if the company wins, cultural scars can remain. Some have attributed the decline of IBM less to the restrictions imposed by the 1956 consent decree and subsequent oversight than to company lawyers' efforts to keep the company out of further trouble. The result was a very legalistic and cumbersome corporate culture that made IBM vulnerable in the marketplace.

If your goal is to delay or block an action, using the courts can be a very useful strategy. The judicial process can be a very effective offensive tool. The optical networking company Ciena, for example, filed a patent-infringement suit against its rival Corvis just a week before Corvis was scheduled to go public; the suit put Corvis' IPO in jeopardy. Regardless of the eventual outcome, Ciena scored a win by interfering with Corvis' plans.[8] Of course, legal action may not work. Intergraph, a small manufacturer of computer workstations, sued Intel for patent infringement, alleging that Intel was using its dominant position in the marketplace to force Intergraph to give up patent rights on certain new chip designs. An Alabama court made a preliminary ruling in favor of Intergraph, but an appeals court subsequently ruled in Intel's favor.[9]

Your involvement in a legal dispute may not be voluntary. Nonbusiness groups initiate legal challenges; regulatory agencies use the courts to enforce regulations, and, as we have just seen, other businesses use the courts to advance their own strategic goals. Despite the eventual outcome, Intergraph's patent-infringement suit against Intel created serious strategic challenges for Intel in the form of an FTC antitrust investigation. Monsanto has been sued by a small group of farmers who alleged that the company had given false guarantees about the safety of its bioengineered seeds. The suit is backed by a coalition of environmental groups, including Greenpeace, and has the potential to travel through multiple levels of the court system.

Refereeing by Regulatory Agencies

Not all refereeing takes place in the judicial branch. Many agencies, such the Internal Revenue Service (IRS), the Environmental Protection Agency (EPA), and the Federal Trade Commission (FTC), have the authority to conduct certain kinds of investigations and to make rulings that bind companies. Regulatory agencies are therefore responsible for enforcing the regulations they write, giving them a unique dual role as rule maker and referee. One commentator has described administrative agencies as a "fourth branch of government," noting that they "perform some of the functions of each of the other three branches, with quasi-legislative and quasi-judicial as well as executive roles."[10]

We have already explored leverage points in agency rule making processes, but the refereeing functions of agencies are equally important to understand and to influence. Routine refereeing—enforcement of OSHA regulations, fines for labor-law violations, implementing a change in emission requirements, and the like—affects business to varying degrees. You should continuously keep tabs on how regulations affect your business, and how your actions could be viewed by regulatory agencies. Once again, becoming complacent about your relationship with government puts your business at risk.

But sometimes the enforcement actions of regulatory agencies can have massive and long-lasting impacts on business, such as when the FTC blocked the merger of WorldCom and Sprint. Regulatory agencies wield a great deal of power in their role as referee:

from imposing fines to filing suit, regulatory agencies can severely impact business in the course of enforcing the rules.

Legislatures confer adjudicative powers on administrative agencies because the courts lack the time and, crucially, the expertise to hear all such cases. Consider, for example, the task of reviewing the thousands of mergers and other cases involving antitrust issues that arise in the United States each year. Responsibility for refereeing antitrust cases falls to the Antitrust Division of the Justice Department (DOJ) and to the FTC. If the Justice Department decides to block or modify a merger and the companies involved will not go along, the DOJ sues in federal court. Antitrust investigations by the FTC, by contrast, are adjudicated by an appointed set of commissioners. Its decisions are, however, potentially subject to judicial review according to standards set by the legislature.

One potential leverage point is decision making about the forum in which your case will be heard. The Antitrust Division of the DOJ and the FTC negotiate over which merger cases they will take in a process called *clearance*. The FTC, for example, was the first agency to review Microsoft's business practices in the early 1990s. When it decided not to proceed, the Antitrust Division took up the case, much to the later chagrin of the FTC. This is why DOJ ended up handling the Microsoft case and FTC the Intel case.

The implication is that you can sometimes engage in *forum shopping:* influencing which forum your case is heard in. Companies seeking to block rivals' mergers, for example, can do the work necessary to build the case and then bring it to the agency they see as most sympathetic to their position. This preparatory work can give the agency the upper hand in the clearance process. As one experienced antitrust attorney put it:

> The people who are successful in provoking agency action are people who by and large come in and say, "Look, here's your theory of harm; here's what you can do." There have been some successful third-party actions to stop mergers where the complainant hired counsel

that basically created the merger screening memo for the [agency] staff person. "Here's what you should argue as to why you need a second request [a request for more extensive information from the companies involved in a merger], and here's what you should try to get, and here's your case." Third parties can make a staff attorney look really good.

Challenging the Rules

The Telecommunications Act of 1996 and the rules it spawned have faced significant legal challenges since passage:

- A suit by the American Civil Liberties Union in Federal District Court challenging the constitutionality of the Communications Decency Act (CDA). The District Court ruled that the CDA was a violation of the First Amendment. The government appealed and the case proceeded to the Supreme Court, which upheld the lower court ruling and declared the CDA unconstitutional in 1997.

- Challenges to the constitutionality of the Telecommunications Act by two Baby Bells, BellSouth and SBC Communications, claiming that the Act unconstitutionally singled them out for punishment by excluding them from the long-distance market until they opened their own local phone markets to competition. The cases went to the Supreme Court, which refused to hear them. This outcome meant that the Baby Bells have to comply with the FCC's tests of what constitutes an open, competitive market.

- Even the authority of the FCC as the appropriate enforcer of the CDA was challenged in court. Immediately after the FCC issued its rules in 1996, GTE and the Baby Bells filed suit to block the FCC's orders. In 1997, the U.S. Court of Appeals threw out the FCC's rules on pricing, restoring pricing authority to the states. The FCC appealed to the Supreme Court, which reinstated the FCC's authority in 1999.

The courts have also been the forums for arguments over enforcement of the law:

- Two separate suits by AT&T alleging that the states of Nebraska and New Jersey impeded AT&T's efforts to compete in local phone markets.

- A lawsuit by CTC Communications charging that Bell Atlantic has conspired to discourage competition to provide local telecom services.

- A suit by a coalition of local and national companies, including AT&T and MCI, to prevent U.S. West from marketing the long-distance services of Qwest Communications on the grounds that U.S. West's local market is not sufficiently open to competition. Partly as a result of this suit, U.S. West made an offer to acquire Qwest, a mega-merger likely to receive FCC approval.

The FCC has also acted as a referee, determining everything from when a Baby Bell could start providing long-distance service to reviewing potential mergers. For example, the FCC recently approved Bell Atlantic's bid to offer long-distance service in New York, declaring that the company had met the requirements for opening up its local market. AT&T immediately filed suit challenging the FCC ruling, claiming that the requirements had not been met.

Coming Full Circle

No good deed goes unpunished. The unresolved issues that were the legacy of the Telecommunications Act of 1996 have become fodder for ongoing efforts to amend and extend telecommunications legislation and to rewrite the rules. The 1999–2000 session of Congress took up, but did not pass, legislation dealing with broadband that would have allowed the Baby Bells to get into long-distance data services. Another bill dealt with ownership of data on the Internet. Observers expect the next Congress to take up both of these issues.

Having an Impact

In summary, there are some critical points to remember about government processes as you begin to craft an influence strategy:

- The legislative, regulatory, and judicial processes constitute an interconnected system. Often their actions in a given sphere are overlapping or simultaneous, and what happens in one arena can influence what happens in the other two. You should pay attention continuously to what's happening in each arena.

- Each process has specific leverage points. Awareness of those points is critical to a successful influence strategy. Choosing your entry points is equally critical.

- You should position yourself to influence multiple points in the process, sometimes simultaneously. You also need back-up plans in case the leverage points you pinpoint shift in response to events.

- Rule making is never over. Even after passage of a law, a bill may be introduced to overturn it. Both legislative and regulatory actions can be challenged in court. Keep on paying attention, because the rules can always change.

Use the worksheet that follows to help you identify key leverage points:

At what levels (local, state, federal, and international) is this game played, or could it be played?

At which one or two of these levels are we most likely to achieve our goal?

What/who are the key points of leverage (processes and decision makers) at each level?

Where do we expect the opposition to focus its attention? How is the opposition likely to respond to our moves?

Equipped with a deeper understanding of government processes, you are now in a position to begin to build supportive coalitions to exert influence at key leverage points. That is the subject of Chapter 6.

CHAPTER 6

Building Coalitions

Whether your goal is to pass legislation or to delay implementation of a new rule, the ability to build coalitions is an essential skill. Coalitions are critical to influence legislators or regulators at all levels of government—local, state, federal, or international. "When business leaders want to encourage government to take action," one government relations professional observes, "what they need to do is create a parade of leaders to lead, to build a foundation in substance and support . . . and to align interests so that the official sees that there is substantial support for the action that is being sought. That makes it easier for the elected official to undertake what is being requested." An experienced lobbyist agreed: "It is very important for us to have a large group of people so we can say to the folks on the Hill, 'There's this big army behind us, and this is what they're looking for.'"

The power of coalition building is apparent in the following examples:

- In May 2000, when the House passed a bill imposing a five-year moratorium on Internet taxes, the forces lobbying to keep the Internet tax-free thought they had the upper hand.[1] Then, unexpectedly, a broad coalition emerged to press for sales taxes on online purchases. In a focused lobbying blitz, the coalition successfully stalled the tax-moratorium legislation and pushed for the introduction of new bills that would begin to apply uniform standards for taxing online purchases. The coalition included brick-and-mortar retailers represented by the National Retailers Association, which attacked tax-free sales as fundamentally unfair, and state and local government workers and teachers' unions fearful of the impact on their members of lost sales-tax revenues. The International Council of Shopping Centers got its members to send hundreds of letters to Congress, commissioned a poll showing that 65 percent of Americans consider it unfair not to apply sales taxes to online merchants, and sponsored ads in Washington newspapers. The president of Rice University and 175 economists lobbied Congress to consider how education would be affected if states lose revenue because of online sales. The opponents of a sales-tax-free Internet formed the E-Fairness Coalition to help coordinate their activities. The outcome is not yet determined, but the momentum created by the anti-tax forces had been decisively blunted.

- In early 2000, U.S. airlines and air-freight carriers undertook a vigorous campaign to win 10 coveted daily round-trip flights between the United States and China.[2] FedEx, United Airlines, and Northwest, which already flew to China, hoped to extend their operations and keep their rivals out of the market. UPS, American, and Delta hoped to gain a foothold and expand their global reach. Decision-making authority rested with a deputy assistant secretary in the Department of Transportation (DOT). The arm's-length application process prohibited contenders from talking directly to DOT, but this did not stop them from pursuing every possible source of political advantage; it was widely understood that political considerations would be one factor in the decision. UPS retained former U.S. Trade Representative Mickey Kantor, and American Airlines garnered the support of 20 senators and Richard Daley, mayor of Chicago and brother of the Secretary of Commerce. The competing carriers urged economists, businesses, and customers to flood DOT with studies and letters supporting their positions. Visitors to American's and Delta's Web sites could send supportive letters to DOT with a few mouse clicks. The contenders also mobilized politicians and residents of communities where they are headquartered. Even nonprofit organizations were mobilized. Project HOPE, a provider of emergency medical relief, backed UPS. In an ironic twist, the Teamsters Union, 200,000 of whose members work at UPS, lobbied on behalf of the company, arguing that awarding it the route would create 1,200 new U.S. jobs. Meanwhile, the Teamsters and most other U.S. unions were seeking to block Chinese admission into the World Trade Organization (WTO). In late 2000, UPS was given the right to make six trips a week while United Airlines added two trips and Northwest and Federal Express each added one.

- In the mid-1980s, the Intellectual Property Committee, a group of 13 CEOs of U.S. pharmaceutical, chemical, software, and entertainment companies, initiated a decade-long effort to strengthen protection for their companies' intellectual property.[3] Firms in these industries were losing billions of dollars to copying of drugs, pesticides, computer programs, and videos in countries like China, Brazil, and India, where copying was legal. International agreements on patents and trademarks, administered by an agency of the United Nations, were largely toothless. The coalition got the issue on the agenda of Congress and persuaded the U.S. Trade Representative to take up their case. Then, working with industry associations in Europe and Japan, they assembled a powerful international coalition of businesses and governments. The coalition succeeded in getting intellectual property on the agenda for the Uruguay Round of the GATT trade negotiations. The result was a 1994 agreement on a sweeping new set of global rules protecting trade in intellectual property.

Each of these initiatives involved multiple groups. Most efforts to influence rule making are similarly complex, and it is often tough to know where to begin to build a coalition. To cut through the fog, you need to assess the situation so you can see who is essential to making things happen—both decision makers and potential allies—and how they can be influenced. You also need coalition-building tools: powerful, generic approaches to alliance building that work in a wide array of situations. Then, you have to organize to implement your strategy. This means tapping into existing organizations, such as trade associations, and sometimes creating whole new institutions, like the Intellectual Property Committee and the E-Fairness Coalition mentioned earlier. A good diagnosis of the situation lays the groundwork for a winning coalition-building strategy. Organizational skill brings the strategy to life.

A Toolbox for Coalition Building

Whatever the situation you face, 10 techniques outlined next constitute a well-equipped toolbox for building coalitions to influence rule makers and referees:

1. *Map the influential players.* Who are the key decision makers? Who holds sway over them? Who are your potential allies and adversaries?

2. *Identify potential alignments.* What foundations can be laid to establish alliances?

3. *Assess winning and blocking coalitions.* Whom do you need to get on board? Which parties seem positioned to coalesce and oppose you?

4. *Shift the balance of forces.* How can you convince the convincible?

5. *Shape the agenda.* How can you define "the problem" favorably?

6. *Alter perceptions of alternatives.* How can you shape others' perceptions of their options?

7. *Exploit the power of deference.* Who influences the people you need to influence?

8. *Leverage the power of commitment.* How can you propel potential allies onto the slippery slope toward commitment?

9. *Set up action-forcing events.* What will induce potential allies to make the necessary tough choices?

10. *Plot out a sequence to build momentum.* What is the best strategy for approaching others?

Technique 1. Map the Influential Players

You cannot tell the players without a program. So the starting point is to be sure you understand who the influential players are. Do not cast your net too narrowly in choosing the players: resist limiting yourself to the existing set. Think who else might get involved to buttress or, alternatively, to undermine your efforts. How might you bring in more supporters, and thereby forestall involvement by potential adversaries?

Your identification of key leverage points should provide insight into which decision makers you should target. Recall, for example, that the Deputy Assistant Secretary of Transportation was responsible for allocating the new air routes to China. Next, think about who holds sway over him. Does he have a champion in Congress, someone who helped him get his political appointment? If so, include that congressman in your influence targeting.

Next, extend your analysis to consider nongovernmental key players. For instance, might other businesses represent potential allies? Take the example of the Intellectual Property Committee's efforts to strengthen international protection for intellectual property. What about other business opponents, as in the case involving Microsoft and its many adversaries? What about public interest organizations—nonprofits like Project Hope, the media, or unions like the Teamsters? In short, think as expansively as possible in mapping out your playing field.

In fact, drawing a map of sorts may be useful. Figure 6.1 shows participants in the competition for new air routes to China.

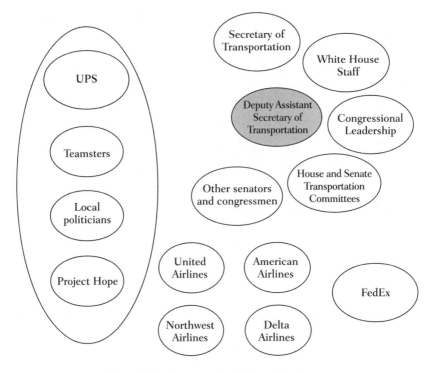

Figure 6.1   Mapping the influential players.

The shaded oval signifies the key leverage point. But keep in mind that other players, both in Congress and the executive branch, may have influence over decision making. Creating a map will stimulate your thinking and help condense information succinctly.

Technique 2. Identify Potential Alignments

There are two primary bases for building alliances: shared interests and complementary goals.[4] The corporate CEOs who created the Intellectual Property Committee were bound (for more than a decade!) by a common interest in protecting their companies' intellectual property.

But not all alliances involve such long-term interests. Powerful alliances can just as easily be built on a foundation of short-term-oriented you-scratch-my-back-and-I'll-scratch-yours arrangements. So, keep this nuance in mind. It can also be worthwhile to engender coalitions involving players with *complementary goals* on specific issues, rather then shared interests per se. Alignments of the latter type can produce strange bedfellows, such as the Teamsters and UPS, or the environmental groups that supported the CSX and Norfolk Southern railway merger discussed earlier.

Sometimes players band together for the sole purpose of combating a common enemy, or denying resources to opponents. The software companies that helped foment the Microsoft antitrust suit were, at one time, fierce competitors; they agreed on practically nothing other than the need to defend themselves against Microsoft's hegemony.

UPS's alliance with the Teamsters in pursuit of China air routes provides another salient example of strange bedfellows. Though in disagreement on the more overarching issue of trade with China, UPS and the Teamsters had the narrower and more immediate common goal of air routes as an incentive to collaborate.

Less obviously, United Airlines and Northwest Airlines were positioned to side with UPS, while American and Delta were apt to be adversarial (and side with FedEx). Why? Because some of the air routes were likely to go to new players, and United and Northwest preferred the new player to be a cargo company rather than another airline. Likewise, FedEx wanted to see the air routes granted to American or Delta rather than to UPS. Thus, while pursuing the routes themselves, it was no less important to keep the competition from gaining ground.

In thinking about alliance creation, bear in mind that such collaborations may be either *explicit* or *tacit*. The fact that it may be dangerous to openly recruit other players does not mean that coalitions cannot be built. While face-to-face discussions might be ideal, *sending the right signals* through action can often be as effective.

Table 6.1 is a worthwhile tool for brainstorming about your web of alliances. Start by laying out the relevant variables. With whom do you have shared interests or complementary goals? Which coalitions can be developed openly and which should be

Table 6.1   Implications of Approach

	Shared Interests	Complementary Goals
Explicit discussions		
Implicit cooperation		

handled with greater delicacy? Once you have identified the various players with whom you will be contending, and how you will be approaching each, check your assessments. As comprehensively as possible, consider the implications of your approach to each prospective alliance.

And is your objective to break opposing alliances, or to prevent them from forming in the first place? Generally speaking, alliances based on deeply shared interests are much more robust than alliances based on complementary goals. Once an alliance founded on shared interests has been formed, it is very difficult to break. Thus, the goal is to deprive opponents with shared interests of the opportunity to organize, perhaps by moving quickly to cement your own coalition. Temporary coalitions based on opportunistic trades are typically held together by the often-tenuous bond of trust among the parties. You may be able to convince certain parties that they would be better off coming over to your side. But the opportunistic alliances you build also will always be vulnerable. This means that maintaining these alliances is as important as building them in the first place.

Technique 3. Assess Winning and Blocking Coalitions

Next, you can deepen your understanding of prospective players by figuring out which players you need to build a *winning coalition*. A winning coalition is best understood as a set of allies with whom you enjoy the critical mass of influence necessary to achieve your goals. According to one trade association member, "You need to build coalitions—to find people who are motivated to support what it is that you want—so that when the government official talks with you, or hears from you, he will recognize that there is a cadre of support for what it is you are seeking." Hardheaded thinking about the composition of a winning coalition will help you to establish priorities for recruiting allies.

This is also the time to identify potential *blocking coalitions,* those that jeopardize your position. Only by identifying potential blocking coalitions can you take action to prevent them from coalescing or, in other cases, to blunt their strategies.

Consider the player map in Figure 6.2, which shows the key governmental participants in the dispute over international protection for intellectual property. To get intellectual property on the agenda for the Uruguay Round of the GATT negotiations, the Intellectual Property Committee (IPC) first had to secure the support of the United States, Japan, and Europe. But the IPC still would not have had a winning coalition; if the developing countries, led by India, Brazil, Egypt, and Pakistan, could recruit a critical mass of others, particularly the newly industrialized economies of the Association of Southeast Asian Nations (ASEAN), they would be able to block action.[5] As this analysis suggests, the ASEAN countries were of pivotal importance. Fortunately for the IPC, the ASEAN group was anxious to protect its access to markets in developed countries and to blunt U.S. ability to apply sanctions unilaterally. They understood that part of the price of U.S. support for a new World Trade Organization (WTO) with dispute-resolution powers was for them to support tighter controls on intellectual property. This linkage of issues ultimately won over the ASEAN countries to the developed-country camp; they then helped mediate an agreement with the developing countries, isolating India. A winning coalition emerged.

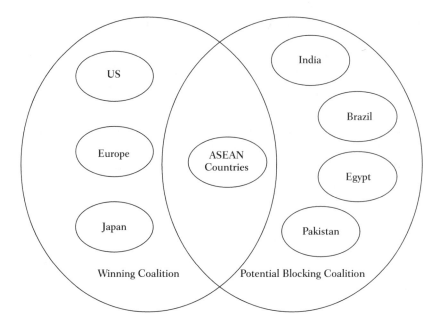

Figure 6.2 ASEAN countries coalition.

For each game you listed earlier, fill out Table 6.2. Brainstorm as freely as possible about allies, adversaries, and those who are on the fence. And think in terms of "strange bedfellows"—people you might not expect to support (or oppose) you on a particular issue. Remember, for instance, that environmental groups supported the merger of railroad giants CSX and Norfolk Southern, and that their support proved critical to the success of the merger.

In analyzing the threat of potential blocking coalitions, try to answer the following questions:

- How long have efforts to organize opposition been under way?

- Is the opposition united by longstanding relationships and shared interests, or by short-term opportunism?

- Are there identifiable linchpins whose conversion or neutralization would substantially weaken resistance?

Table 6.2 Allies and Adversaries

	Who?	Interests?
Potential allies		
Potential adversaries		
On the fence		

This analysis will help you assess the risk that a potent opposing coalition will form. It will also clarify whether to focus on preventing formation of a blocking coalition, such as preemptively recruiting pivotal parties, or to blunt the efforts of an existing coalition by framing more persuasive messages aimed at key decision makers.

Technique 4. Shift the Balance of Forces

Some allies will sign on early and easily because supporting your agenda advances their own interests in ways that are immediately clear to them. In such cases, it is simply a matter of communicating and coordinating with them. Other parties will oppose your efforts regardless of what you do. U.S. business was never going to convince the Indian government that stronger protection for intellectual property was a good idea. Time and resources should not be wasted on the irrevocably opposed, so it is essential to assess early on who is likely to be supportive, who will oppose you no matter what, and who is convincible.

Having identified some key players as convincible, you can gain insight into how they are persuaded by analyzing the *driving and restraining forces* acting on them. Driving forces push potential allies in your direction; restraining forces push them to join the opposing camp or remain uncommitted. Players typically become fenced in because they are experiencing opposing pressures.[6] The source of tension might be internal conflicts (Do we want X more than Y? Should we do what we *want* to do or what we think we *should* do?) or external pressures such as commitments to longstanding existing allies.[7] The forces acting on the ASEAN countries in the debate over global intellectual-property protection, for example, are illustrated in the *force-field diagram* in Figure 6.3.

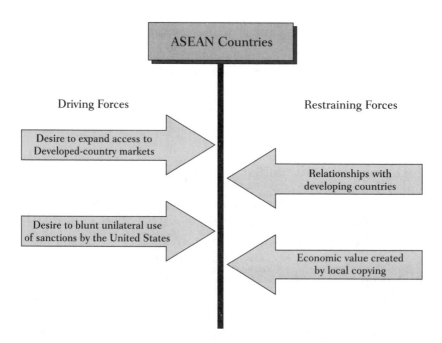

Figure 6.3 ASEAN country driving/restraining forces.

It is often surprising to do a force-field analysis for each party you need to convince. Your goal, after all, is to alter the balance of forces acting on them: strengthening the forces driving them in your direction, weakening the restraining forces, or both. The driving forces acting on the ASEAN countries, for example, were strengthened by U.S. legislation authorizing unilateral trade sanctions to punish countries that did not protect intellectual property. Partially in response to complaints from pharmaceutical makers, the United States took steps toward imposing sanctions on Korea, thus putting other countries on notice. Other approaches to shifting the balance of forces include shaping the agenda, altering perceptions of alternatives, and exploiting patterns of deference.

Technique 5. Shape the Agenda

"Pay great attention to the agenda of the debate," cautions Owen Harries, an expert on legislative maneuver. "He who defines the issues and determines their priority is already well on the way to winning."[8] Thus, one key to coalition building is simply to be there during the formative period—to define the terms of the debate before momentum builds in the wrong direction. For example, the Intellectual Property Committee helped shape the agenda for the upcoming debate. During the lead-up to substantive negotiations over international intellectual property, the IPC took advantage of two years of procedural wrangling to clarify its position, do supporting analysis, and compose a position statement.

IPC intellectual-property specialists also met with their counterparts in Japanese and European trade associations to begin drafting a proposed framework agreement. Explained a leader of this effort: "We basically wanted to come up with a book that said, 'This is what we want.'" The result was a 100-page document spelling out the minimum standards for an acceptable agreement on the trade-related aspects of intellectual-property rights. This unique collaboration among the U.S., European, and Japanese business communities was characterized by Hewlett-Packard president and CEO John A. Young as "unprecedented . . . the first time that the international business community has jointly developed a document of this magnitude and such substantive detail for presentation to our government negotiators."[9] The report ultimately functioned as one of two prototypes for the final agreement. It is often possible to get the jump on others by getting something into writing.

Sometimes you can broaden your coalition by adding issues to the agenda. Protecting intellectual property, for example, got linked to the broader issue of foreign investment: The IPC promoted the idea that developing countries' support for strengthening intellectual-property protection was a litmus test for foreign investment. Developing countries were made to see intellectual-property protection as the price of new dispute-resolution forums and rules in the World Trade Organization (WTO).

Agenda setting may also involve excluding toxic issues or setting them aside for later on. The United States, the EU, and Japan, for example, disagreed about the *specific changes* required to strengthen intellectual-property protection. Rather than argue about it and undermine their efforts, they worked to identify the baseline characteristics that their patent, copyright, and trademark regimes shared. They then codified these features into a set of *basic principles* around which they could rally. Only after they had won the basic dispute with the developing countries did they hash out their own differences. As one leader of the IPC effort noted, "We didn't say, in terms of patents, that it had to be a first-to-file system as opposed to a first-to-invent system. We just said that every country has to have a system for giving a patent."[10]

Like all the techniques we have discussed, management of the agenda can also be used to pressure opposing coalitions. You may, for example, be able to add an issue to the agenda that divides your opponents. Even the order in which issues are addressed is important. Beginning with a contentious issue can forestall formation of a blocking coalition; conversely, beginning with an issue on which you and potential allies agree may help to seal a winning coalition.

Finally, efforts to shape the agenda are often built on effective *framing* of persuasive messages. Framing is itself a big topic—so big, in fact, that we will devote the next chapter to it.

Technique 6. Alter Perceptions of Alternatives

Another way to tip the balance of forces is to make potential allies' alternatives to supporting you seem less attractive. Each potential ally has a "best alternative" to an alliance with you; it may be to remain uncommitted or to join an opposing coalition.[11] You have to convince each one that supporting you (or at least not opposing you) is the preferred alternative. This is the art of choice-shaping.

Carrots and sticks are standard tools for changing potential allies' perceptions of their alternatives; they are, respectively, the push and pull of influence strategy. In the intellectual-property debate, for example, the United States offered developing countries the carrot of access to markets for their textile and agricultural products. But the United States also wielded the stick of sanctions. Developing countries objected to cross-sanctions—trade reprisals for breaches of intellectual-property protection under the WTO—but came to see them as preferable to answering exclusively to the United States.

Another way to shape choices is to convince potential allies that the status quo is no longer an option. When asked to decide between perpetuating a comfortable status quo or striking off in potentially unnerving new directions, people usually opt for familiarity. If the status quo is not viable, however, the other alternatives become more plausible and attractive. The power of eliminating the status quo is illustrated by the experience of a worker on an offshore oil platform that suddenly caught fire. He ran to the edge of the platform, peered down at the churning ocean 150 feet below, and hesitated. Then he turned and saw a ball of fire approaching. As the fire was about to engulf him, he jumped—and survived. You do not need to create a crisis to gain support, although it sometimes works to do so. The point is that eliminating the option of staying put is a powerful persuasion tool.

A related technique is to convince potential allies that you will move ahead with or without them. To carry this off, you have to be able to credibly threaten to act unilaterally. Suppose you are deciding whether to recruit allies or act on your own. If you are unlikely to succeed alone, potential allies have significant power in their negotiations with you: their support is necessary, and they can extract value in exchange for that support. They may thus claim a disproportionate share of the spoils of success or "water down" your goals.

Now suppose you have a reasonable chance of success alone (or with existing support). Your very ability to proceed alone can persuade potential allies to join your coalition. Everyone wants to jump on the bandwagon, because they realize that it is better to be inside than out in the cold. As one CEO observes, "No one will take the first step forward, but if someone else takes that first step, then no one wants to get left out."

This is why experienced coalition builders work at maintaining the credibility of their options to act unilaterally. If you repeatedly threaten unilateral action but never follow through, your credibility will suffer. Of course, going it alone can also lead to problems. Overdependence on allies can lead to paralysis, but overuse of unilateral action may lead to isolation.

Technique 7. Exploit the Power of Deference

Decision makers are usually enmeshed in networks of relationships that shape their actions. Virtually every government decision maker or potential ally has someone from whom they request advice, or to whom deference or obligation is due. It is often possible to discern who influences a potential ally, and who in turn influences the influencers. Such analysis can equip you to use social influence to tip the balance of forces.

It is also worth the time to map out *influence networks*—established patterns of deference on key issues.[12] This means figuring out existing deference patterns and identifying points where it is possible to *indirectly* exert influence over others. Even if you have no direct relationship with a potential ally, you may still be able to work indirectly through *bridging players*—people who have some influence over target allies and whom you in turn can influence.

Early in the IPC's campaign to build a coalition, for example, U.S. Trade Representative Clayton Yeutter advised them to solicit support internationally in order to overcome resistance. In mid-1986, IPC representatives spent three months travelling to Tokyo, Bonn, London, Paris, Brussels, and Copenhagen to make their case. Ultimately, the IPC formed a tripartite coalition with the European Union of Industrial and Employers' Confederations and a powerful federation of economic organizations in Japan. These organizations worked as bridging parties to convince their governments that intellectual property should be on the agenda for the GATT talks.

In campaigns to shape public opinion, you can use a similar approach to identify and influence *opinion leaders:* individuals who exert disproportionate influence on wide audiences.[13] We often look to those whom we respect for guidance about "right thinking." Opinion leaders may be distinguished by their expertise or experience, access to information, or simply authoritative personalities. Whatever the source of their stature, it is important to understand how members of your target audiences formulate their opinions about the issues in question. You can try to influence the public directly, through advertising and public relations. But tailoring messages for opinion leaders typically translates into broader acceptance.

Technique 8. Leverage the Power of Commitment

A potential ally who can be induced to make small and apparently innocuous commitments of support has already started down the slippery slope to making much more extensive commitments. This approach to coalition-building, which we call *entanglement,* builds on the observed truth that people can be led from neutrality to full commitment in a succession of small, irreversible steps, when doing so in a single leap would be impossible.

This approach works, in part, because people feel the need to maintain consistency between their commitments and their actions. Social psychologists have demonstrated that living up to commitments, especially those made in public, serves to maintain the image that we want others to have of us. Subsequent actions are taken to maintain consistency (or at least the appearance of consistency) with this image. According to Robert Cialdini, an expert on persuasion, "Once we have made a choice, or taken a stand, we will encounter personal and interpersonal pressures to behave consistently with that commitment."[14]

The implication for coalition building is that asking allies for trivial gestures of support can soften them up for larger commitments; they become entangled in your purposes. The initial commitment allows the prospective ally to easily demonstrate willingness to help. Later requests draw on the need to maintain consistency with this image, which creates barriers to backsliding.

The entanglement strategy also works because no single request is significant enough to provoke much resistance. The building of the Gulf War coalition in 1991 offers a classic example of entanglement from the realm of diplomacy. When Iraq invaded Kuwait, U.S. Secretary of State James Baker asked the Soviets to jointly sponsor a UN resolution condemning the aggression. Once they had agreed to do so, the Soviet leadership had a stake in continuing to be seen as protectors of "the New World Order." The Bush administration was thus able to convince them to go along with an embargo, then a naval blockade, and finally direct military action. The Soviets would certainly never have agreed up-front to an American-led invasion of such an important client state.

When you employ entanglement strategies, keep in mind that public commitments carry more weight than private ones. Commitments made privately afford wiggle room; you can argue that you were misunderstood or misquoted. Backing away from commitments made in front of others is significantly harder: Your reputation is on the line.

The downside of commitments, of course, is that potential allies may already have made them to others. So you should be prepared to help them find convincing rationales for gracefully disentangling themselves and saving face.

Technique 9. Set Up Action-Forcing Events

It can be painful for uncommitted players to decide whom to support, comparable to having to choose sides in a family quarrel

when doing so will inevitably damage certain relationships. For this reason, players may prefer to remain uncommitted as long as they can. Part of your job as a coalition builder is thus to set up *action-forcing events* that impel potential allies to make the necessary tough choices. To put it another way, what prevents key players from stalling, delaying, stonewalling, obfuscating, and generally doing nothing? Players on the horns of a dilemma make hard choices only when they lack more attractive alternatives *and* when doing nothing is not an option. As long as they believe that the costs of action outweigh the potential benefits of inaction, they cannot be expected to act. Coalition building, therefore, often calls for strategic efforts to eliminate "do nothing" as an option.

Action-forcing events, like deadlines, are "break points" that compel players to act to avoid incurring irreversible costs. In the GATT negotiations over intellectual property, the approaching expiration of the Clinton Administration's "fast-track" authority to negotiate trade agreements acted as an action-forcing event. Congress had agreed to strict limits on its ability to modify trade agreements once the president negotiated them. Any agreement had to be considered in its entirety in an up-or-down vote and was not subject to the usual renegotiation or amendment. If the president's fast-track authority expired and was not renewed (which in fact happened), what were the implications? Other nations would justifiably fear that Congress would modify provisional agreements; thus they would be likely to negotiate defensively, never willing to make their final concessions, and probably not reach agreement at all. So the deadline for expiration of the Administration's fast-track mandate focused the minds of the other participants in the GATT negotiations. The result was an agreement before the deadline.

Even when others impose action-forcing events, you may be able to shape those events to impel your coalition-building efforts forward. In Congress, the scheduling of key votes is a tool the leadership uses to force members to commit themselves. You, in turn, may be able to influence this scheduling.

Technique 10. Sequence to Build Momentum

Finally, a coalition-building strategy consists of a sequence of moves.[15] Skilled coalition builders develop *sequencing plans* to propel the process in the desired direction and to build momentum to overwhelm the opposition.

Careful thinking about the order in which you approach potential allies can have an especially powerful impact in coalition building. Once you have one ally, it typically becomes easier to recruit others (unless they are incompatible). As you recruit more allies, your resource base grows and your likelihood of prevailing increases, making it easier to recruit still more supporters.

Effective sequencing transforms uncommitted parties' perceptions of their alternatives. Before your coalition is built, their options are to join your coalition or to maintain the status quo. Once you have accumulated a critical mass of support, they face a very different choice: Join the coalition or be left behind. Sequence matters because uncommitted parties' assessments of your coalition's chances of success are influenced by who has already joined (or refused to). As more parties join, membership in the coalition becomes attractive to more risk-averse players. Ultimately, a threshold is crossed and wholesale movement to the winning side takes place as parties jump on the bandwagon.

The place to begin is to cement your core supporters and then sequence outward, exploiting patterns of deference and getting those you recruit to recruit others. The Intellectual Property Committee, for example, was born out of discussions between the chairman of Pfizer, Edmund Pratt, and IBM chairman John Opel. Both served on the President's Advisory Committee on Trade Negotiations during the Carter and Reagan Administrations. Pratt had chaired the committee; Opel served as head of the intellectual-property task force. "Both of them had problems with piracy and theft of their intellectual property," recalls one U.S. negotiator, "and they decided to get intellectual property into the trade venue where you had some teeth in the enforcement mechanism."[16]

They began by recruiting like-minded CEOs to form the IPC and staff it with industry experts who would form the core of the organization. They then contacted other industry groups with a stake in intellectual-property protection, such as the Anti-Counterfeiting Coalition, a group led by Levi Strauss and other trademark-based companies such as Samsonite, Izod, Chanel, and Gucci.[17]

They also reached out to key people in government. As former CEO of the maker of Yale locks, Commerce Secretary Malcolm Baldrige had an interest in intellectual property; patents had been important to his company's business. Baldrige established an interagency intellectual-property committee. As we have seen, U.S. Trade Representative Clayton Yeutter advised Opel and Pratt to solicit support internationally.

Avoiding the Pitfalls

The 10 tools described in this chapter can be applied to any coalition-building situation. How you put them to use is a matter of judgment. Here are some guidelines to help you avoid some common pitfalls.

Anticipate What Your Adversaries Will Do

You are unlikely to be the only one building coalitions; think a few steps ahead and put yourself in your adversaries' shoes. This is particularly important when you are creating sequencing plans. Your opponents may well be seeking to influence the same set of convincible players, and may be making their own sequencing choices. Your sequencing plans may thus interact, resulting in competition for the support of pivotal players. The ability to be the *first mover* is an important source of advantage. Try to anticipate others' moves and get there first. Once your opponents secure commitments of support, the battle is uphill.

Avoid Provoking Reactive Coalition Building

Sometimes the best approach is to let sleeping dogs lie. Aggressive efforts to build coalitions can trigger equal and opposite reactions if your opponents feel threatened and begin to mobilize. Sometimes this is simply unavoidable. It is always worth asking: Will the benefits of fighting a particular battle or taking an early stand outweigh the costs of putting adversaries on notice and giving them a cause to rally around?

Avoid Making Your Coalition-Building Tactics an Issue

The use of illegitimate tactics in coalition building can easily backfire. In the worst case, your efforts themselves will become the subject of media attention and public criticism. The classic example is Microsoft, whose efforts to channel funding to "independent" groups[18] and to rally congressional support for cutting the budget of the Antitrust Division of the Justice Department were exposed and harshly criticized.

Work to Sustain Your Coalition

Building a coalition is only half the battle; you need to sustain it too. Otherwise support could slip away in the night. Sustaining your coalition means staying in regular communication with your allies and continually working to bolster their support. Says an experienced coalition builder, "Preaching to the converted, far from being a superfluous activity, is vital. Preachers do it every Sunday." Strengthening the commitment, intellectual performance, and morale of those already on your side is an essential task, both in order to bind them more securely to the cause and to make them more effective proponents of it.[19] To sustain its business coalition in the United States, for example, the IPC met with over 30 industry associations every six to nine months to review progress and plan strategy.

Remember That Today's Adversary Is Tomorrow's Ally

The corollary of "politics makes strange bedfellows" is that players frequently shift from bed to bed. So do not burn your bridges unnecessarily, and be careful to avoid turning political differences into personal animosities. The cost of winning a battle can be very high if it damages your reputation and makes future cooperation with influential players impossible. Your coalition-building efforts should build relationship capital, or at least not squander it.

Developing Persuasive Messages

The ultimate goal in coalition building is to convince a critical mass of the convincible to come over to your side. The techniques presented in this chapter give you most of the tools you need to accomplish this. But one element of coalition building, the framing of persuasive messages, is so central to success that the next chapter is devoted entirely to it.

CHAPTER 7

Framing Arguments

Success in building coalitions rests on a foundation of persuasive arguments. If you fail to develop compelling arguments, nothing else you do will have much impact.

The art of framing arguments consists of developing rationales and presenting information in the best possible light to achieve your goals. The messages you create should communicate the right tone, appeal to your audience's values, and resonate with their interests, but it is essential not to step over the line. Framing is not lying or misleading. In fact, shading the truth is the easiest way to lose credibility in the influence game. As one former member of Congress remarks:

> There is a proper term for a lobbyist who lies or misleads or distorts, and that proper term is *former lobbyist*. When you are dealing with each other—member dealing with member, lobbyist dealing with member—the truth is your absolute. That's the real capital. Once you mislead, once you exaggerate, once you fail to give an accurate picture, you'll never be allowed in the office again.

Understanding Framing

Framing is the use of argument, analogy, and metaphor to create a favorable definition of the problem to be solved and the set of acceptable solutions. Framing works because (1) people tend to postpone hardheaded assessments of what is at stake until they actually have to make a choice, and (2) their decisions are influenced by how the available options are posed to them. Deliberately or not, you frame messages every day of your life. How do you advocate for change in your organization? How will you position the launch of a new product? How will you convince your family to vacation at the beach? In these and myriad other situations, you tailor messages to persuade a specific audience. This is the art of framing.

Consider these three examples of effective framing in influencing rule making:

1. During their lobbying blitz in opposition to a tax-free Internet, members of the National Retail Federation met with key congressional aides. In a typical meeting Robert Benham, owner of an Oklahoma City clothing store, met with Dan Barron, an aide to Senator James Inhofe of Oklahoma. "We're not seeking a new tax," he told Barron. "What we are seeking is a level playing field. . . . We're the ones who sponsor the Little League teams, who buy tables at charity events. . . . When's the last time a dot-com did a charity fashion show in your district?"[1]

2. In early 2000, Ford Motor Company launched an unprecedented dialogue with environmental groups. This effort at rapprochement was stimulated in part by environmentalists' attacks on sport utility vehicles (SUVs), which were classified as trucks and hence exempt from the stricter fuel-economy standards applied to cars. The industry was hoping to avoid reclassification of SUVs, but environmentalists and their allies had been gaining ground in the debate. Environmentalists had dubbed Ford's largest SUV, the Excursion, the "Ford Valdez" after the grounded Exxon supertanker that caused widespread

damage in Alaska's Prince William Sound. In July 2000, Ford announced a shift in strategy, committing to improve mileage by five miles per gallon within five years. Weeks later, GM upped the ante, announcing that overall fuel consumption for all its light trucks, including SUVs, would be better than Ford's by 2005.[2]

3. In 1995, the environmental organization Greenpeace prevented Shell Oil from dumping an obsolete oil platform, the Brent Spar, in the North Atlantic. Shell had performed extensive environmental-impact analyses and received permission from the British government to sink the platform in 6,000 feet of water. Shell and other oil companies hoped to dispose of other aging platforms in the same way. Then Greenpeace staged a commando-like boarding of the abandoned platform and created a media circus. Greenpeace also promoted a European boycott of Shell and issued a report alleging that Shell had underestimated the amount of dangerous material, including toxic metals and radioactive sludge, to be dumped. Greenpeace activists cast the controversy in terms easily understood by the public. Why, they asked, should a rich multinational oil company be allowed to dump the platform in the sea when "no one had been able to dump their rusty old car in the local pond for more than 30 years?" This formulation struck a chord with the public, especially in Great Britain. Greenpeace's data on potential environmental risks was later proved to be completely incorrect, and the organization's credibility with the media suffered. But the public outcry had lost Shell the support of the British government. The company had to substitute a more costly (both economically and environmentally) method of disposing of the platform.[3]

In all three cases, effective rhetorical framing played a decisive role in shifting the balance of forces acting on decision makers. By capturing the essence of their arguments in memorable, evocative catch phrases, skillful players were able to shape public opinion and hence bring pressure to bear on rule makers.

Pathways to Persuasion: Interests, Drives, and Mental Models

The essential questions in framing are: Who is the audience and what kinds of arguments will its members find persuasive? Carefully targeting your audience is the obvious starting point, and the tools presented in Chapter 6 for identifying convincibles, doing influence mapping, and pinpointing opinion leaders will help you to do so. The next step is to develop persuasive messages for each audience. The goal here is to help tip the balance of forces so that convincibles line up on your side.

To develop persuasive messages, you will need more than a superficial understanding of the target audience. The people you are trying to persuade are not blank slates. They have *interests* they are seeking to advance, *motivational drives* that impel them in particular directions, and preexisting *mental models* that powerfully shape their judgments. You need to understand not just what they care about, but how they think. Only then can you identify promising pathways to persuasion.

Interests are the goals that people seek to advance. Complex sets of interests often underlie the simple positions that people take on issues: They hew to their positions because they see doing so as the only way to advance their interests. A classic example of this is the negotiations between the Egyptians and the Israelis at Camp David over the future of the Sinai Peninsula.[4] The parties took incompatible positions: Egypt wanted all of its territory back while Israel wanted to retain a buffer zone. But the parties' underlying interests turned out to be compatible: Egypt's primary interest was sovereignty, while Israel's was security. The Camp David treaty returned sovereignty of the Sinai to Egypt but made large portions demilitarized zones and set up a U.N. buffer force in the middle.

The implication is that *reframing*—crafting messages that show people different ways of advancing their interests—can sometimes get them to shift off their positions. This is more likely if you can give people a face-saving path for backing away.

Motivational drives are inner psychological needs that, consciously or unconsciously, shape people's perceptions of their interests. Often these drives have as much to do with process (how will I look and feel if things go that way?) as they do with substance (what will the outcome be?). In assessing the motivational drives of those you seek to influence, be sure to think in terms of:

- *Maintaining control.* Do they need to feel competent, in control, and not controlled by others?

- *Exercising power.* Do they need to "win" or dominate others, and perhaps to demonstrate that they have done so?

- *Maintaining reputation.* Are they concerned about maintaining their reputations (such as for toughness)?

- *Being consistent.* Is it important to them to maintain consistency with prior commitments or statements of principle?[5]

- *Preserving relationships.* Do they regard it as important to preserve relationships or be liked by others?

Though they often function as barriers to persuasion, people's motivational drives can also present opportunities to influence. For instance, persuading a potential ally with a high need for consistency to make a public commitment of support creates a potent barrier to backsliding. Likewise, offering a decision maker preoccupied with his reputation a face-saving way to back you can help neutralize opposition.

Mental models are the preexisting frameworks that people use to make sense of the world.[6] Mental models serve to interpret our observations and experiences, and thus help us figure out what to do in novel situations. They provide the rules of thumb and scripts that guide our actions. Mental models are products of our formative experiences. They embody our values and our beliefs about cause-and-effect relationships and the lessons of history.[7] Without mental models, we would have to figure out every new situation from scratch.

Here again, when it comes to framing persuasive messages, your target audience's mental models can represent either barriers or opportunities. Consider, for example, how the mental models of business executives and union leaders influence their views of free trade. It is relatively easy to convince most businesspeople of the merits of free trade, in part because it is consistent with their interests. But they also view free trade through the lens of the success of trade liberalization in expanding global commerce, the persuasive arguments of leading economists, and the disastrous history of protectionism during the Depression. For union leaders, by contrast, free trade evokes their experiences of downward pressure on wages and loss of jobs to foreign competition.

The mental models that people use to interpret reality are so deeply embedded in their psyches that they are often unaware of their biases. As a result, people commonly block out information that is inconsistent with their mental models—a process known as *selective perception*. People also tend to actively seek evidence that confirms their beliefs.[8] For example, a group engaged in a prolonged conflict is more likely to suspect that an offer by the other side has an ulterior motive than to accept that the "bad guys" would actually make a concession. This tendency makes it easier to play defense than offense in dealing with government: It is a simpler matter to solidify opposition by reinforcing existing mental models than it is to change minds.

The early information that people receive about a situation influences which mental models get activated, and therefore what they think is at stake. The art of framing thus consists in part in crafting arguments that tap into particular preconceived beliefs and attitudes, highlighting some and leaving others dormant. This means two things: First, as Will Rogers so aptly put it, "You never get a second chance at a first impression." Second, your messages should link your position either to values that your audience holds dear or to formative experiences that have powerfully shaped their attitudes.

The use of metaphor and analogy is a powerful way to tap into guiding beliefs and values. Advertisers and propagandists have long since learned the value of linking choices to positive self-definitions. This is why, for example, cigarette advertising features images of beauty and freedom, and why the abortion debate pits life against choice. Likewise, opponents of U.S. intervention abroad invoke the Vietnam quagmire as a potent analogy supporting isolationism, while supporters resurrect the ghost of Hitler to support intervention.

Winning the Frame Game

It is unquestionably important to analyze your audience in order to develop persuasive messages; it is equally important to shape how they perceive their *choices* in the first place (Table 7.1). As we saw in Chapter 6, agenda setting is an essential dimension of coalition building that is easy to overlook. Much can be won or lost early in the game, when the problem and the alternatives get defined. By the time the issues and the options have been framed, the actual outcome may be a foregone conclusion. So it is important to think through how you will win the frame game early on (Table 7.2).

Table 7.1 Assessing Your Audience

Take a minute to think about an individual or group you are trying to persuade to support your position on an important issue. Then answer the following questions:

Concerning interests

What positions have they taken or would they be likely to take on the issues at hand?

What interests underlie those positions?

Can the situation be framed (or reframed) in ways that would allow them to satisfy those interests and still support your position?

Concerning motivational drives

Do they care deeply about control? Power? Reputation? Consistency? Relationships?

How might the process threaten or nourish these underlying psychological needs?

Does a face-saving way exist for them to back away from their current position?

Concerning mental models

What formative experiences have shaped their view of the world?

What values do they hold dear?

What analogies or metaphors do they find persuasive?

Table 7.2   Diagnosing Dominant Frames

Take a few minutes to think about an influence game that you have observed or participated in (not necessarily involving government) and answer the following questions:

What competing frames were individuals or groups promoting?

How did the basic issue or problem get defined? When did this occur? Who exerted influence at that stage and how?

How did the alternatives get defined? When, by whom, and how?

Framing is a particularly potent tool whenever key decision makers have not fully formulated what is at stake and whenever your opponents have not fully developed their positions. By providing a compelling frame of reference that defines the problem, and a set of criteria for distinguishing "good" outcomes from "bad" ones, you can gain advantage at the start.

For example, in its coalition-building efforts in support of international protection for intellectual property, described in Chapter 6, the Intellectual Property Committee dubbed the unauthorized copying of products in developing countries "intellectual piracy." This was actually a mischaracterization, since countries like India, Brazil, and China imposed no legal restrictions on copying, but the image of pirates pillaging and carrying away spoils resonated for many people, including leaders of the U.S. Congress. It was cited extensively, without comment, by leading media publications in the United States and Europe.

Naturally, your opponents will also be trying to frame the terms. Thus, the preliminary stage of an influence game typically consists of a competition to establish the *dominant frame* through which target audiences (decision makers and those who influence them) come to view the issue. Sometimes this calls for researching and writing detailed position papers outlining a favorable framing of the problem and the options. At other times, or simultaneously, framing involves the persuasive use of language. Which is more resonant, pro-life or pro-choice? Is the debate to be framed in terms of estate taxes or death taxes?

Rules of Framing

Framing is an art, not a science. Nevertheless, here are seven tried-and-true rules to guide the development of persuasive messages.

Rule 1: Make Your Issue Their Issue

You have specific interests you hope to advance. But it is essential to translate or interpret the situation in such a way that key decision makers and those who influence them can see how it will (or could) affect them. To do so, you need to understand your audience at a deep level. Only by fully understanding their interests (and the drives and mental models that influence them) can you hope to frame the issue and options in a way that will make the impact on their interests clear. Linking undesirable policy options to the possibility of a recession, for example, is much more persuasive to someone who lived through the double-digit inflation of the late 1970s than to someone who has never experienced inflation above 3 percent. Again, framing messages that affirm core values and create potent images calls for knowing your audience.

Another effective way to make your issue their issue is to use data and analysis. Consider the efforts of the Health Industry Manufacturers Association (HIMA) to avoid deep cuts in reimbursement for medical devices in Japan in the mid-1990s. HIMA feared that the Japanese government was specifically targeting the U.S. medical-devices industry. A Japanese government agency released a report purporting to prove that prices for U.S.-made medical devices were much higher in Japan than in other markets. The report was picked up by the Japanese press and used as an opportunity to portray U.S. companies as "foreign price gougers." In response, HIMA commissioned its own study to reframe the debate in terms of innovation and the total cost of treating an illness, rather than the cost of individual devices. The HIMA report also showed that the cost differences were largely attributable to inefficiencies in the Japanese health-care system. This data provided support for Japanese advocates of health-care reform, who became an important set of allies for HIMA.[9]

Rule 2: Make the Specific General and the General Specific

Sometimes it is best to frame choices in broad general terms (for instance, this is good for the environment); at other times, a specific narrow focus is best (this will decrease pollution in the river that flows through your state capital). An option that could attract undesirable outside support or opposition should be framed as an isolated case, not precedent setting. But if you are trying to build a coalition around a narrow local issue, you may be able to attract broader support by framing it as setting a precedent (desirable or undesirable) that will promote or block similar initiatives elsewhere.

In July 2000, for example, environmental groups succeeded in getting Smithfield Foods, a North Carolina pig-farming company, to sign an agreement with the state to mitigate the impact of open-lagoon treatment of animal waste on the environment. The flooding caused by Hurricane Floyd the previous year had caused waste from dozens of these open pits to flow into local rivers, raising public awareness of the issue. Environmental groups such as the Sierra Club targeted Smithfield because it was the world's largest pork producer. They garnered nationwide support for their efforts by arguing that the case would set a crucial precedent for future battles with the industry, both within the state and elsewhere. After being slapped with lawsuits, Smithfield agreed to fund a two-year $15 million North Carolina State University study to test alternative waste-treatment technologies on a commercial scale and to contribute $50 million over 25 years for an environmental fund. Under the agreement, this initiative will lead to a phase out of open-air lagoons. "What happened in North Carolina today may have major national implications down the road," said Ed Hopkins, the Sierra Club's senior Washington representative, of the victory. "We look forward to an industrywide switch to improved technology which will result in cleaner air and water in North Carolina and around the country."[10]

Rule 3: Take Advantage of Characteristic Biases in How People Make Decisions

Research has shown consistent biases in how people evaluate situations and make decisions.[11] Two biases that come into play in influencing government are *loss aversion* and *risk aversion.*

Loss aversion is what it sounds like; people typically care more deeply about avoiding losses than they do about achieving equivalent gains. Research has shown that people view losses and gains very differently, and that those differences affect how they make decisions. This means that:

- You should emphasize the benefits of a desired course of action, and minimize its costs. If your goal is to block an initiative, you should do the exact opposite.

- A gain has inherent value for people regardless of its size; a loss, in and of itself, is experienced as a privation. This means that you should unbundle the benefits and present each separately, while bundling costs to lessen their cumulative impact.

Most people are *risk-averse:* in a choice between a sure gain and a risky bet, the bet must have a significantly greater expected value than the sure gain (this is known as a *risk premium*) to be chosen. At the same time, people are notoriously bad at assessing the probabilities of potential outcomes. When framing issues with uncertain outcomes, you can therefore take advantage of risk aversion by emphasizing the riskiness of an undesirable course of action and downplaying the risks of your preferred course of action.

Biases like loss aversion and risk aversion are another reason why it is easier to play defense than offense. The gains associated with change are often uncertain and remote in time, while the losses may be immediate and painful. Likewise, change often promises to yield small benefits for many people but large losses for a few, who mobilize vigorously to oppose it. Free trade is a classic example.

Rule 4: Inoculate the Audience against Expected Challenges

As far back as Aristotle, persuaders have been advised to inoculate their audiences against the expected arguments of their opponents. In any debate over legislation or regulation, there is always another side. By refuting the opposition's probable arguments early on, you effectively inoculate your audience.

Consider the excerpt from Philip Morris' tobacco business Web site in Figure 7.1.[12] How is the company attempting to frame the policy issues? What opposing arguments is it trying to anticipate and counter?

A Few Thoughts Regarding Cigarettes and Adult Choice

As a responsible cigarette manufacturer, we believe in the principle of adult choice. Although the particulars of the public policy issues regarding our product may differ from place to place and from time to time, Internet technology has now given us the opportunity to assemble, in a convenient and easily accessible format, overviews and ideas (many of them competing) about a number of issues concerning smoking and health.

These include issues that have been widely discussed in societies around the world, such as "secondhand" smoke, tar and nicotine, addiction and disease. In addition, there are many aspects of modern cigarettes and tobacco regulation that may interest you: the ingredients that are added; the differences between "full-flavor" and "light" brands; and quitting smoking are just a few examples. We've attempted to organize these pages so as to give you easy access to a wide range of information and opinion about these topics.

Cigarettes are a legal product that many adults enjoy, notwithstanding the serious health issues surrounding smoking. Although it is appropriate for governments and health authorities to encourage people to avoid risky behaviors, we don't believe that they should *prohibit* adults from choosing to smoke. The decision as to whether or not to smoke should be left to individual adults.

Figure 7.1   Philip Morris example: Why discuss tobacco issues?

Another example (Figure 7.2) is drawn from Philip Morris' policy statement on marketing to minors.[13] Once again, what arguments is the company trying to anticipate?

The last link provides some insight into why the company is seeking to frame the debate in the way it is. The linked study by Monitoring the Future of youth smoking in the United States reveals that 54.8 percent of eighth grade students who smoked used Philip Morris products. The numbers were higher in grades 10 and 12, 67.2 percent and 66.9 percent, respectively.[14]

Rule 5: Focus and Repeat

Research on persuasive communication attests to the power of messages that are focused and repeated.[15] People who try to communicate too much information at once end up confusing their audiences and not communicating anything. An effectively framed message is like a song with a catchy tune: Once you hear it a couple of times, you cannot get it out of your mind. Take the American Express slogan "Don't leave home without it." You may not have heard it for years, but it probably sticks in your mind and may have established a persistent association.

With sufficient focus and repetition, a resonant message can become viral—that is, it can spread without much additional effort on your part. A well-framed message does not just influence its immediate target; it also provides a persuasive script for convincing others.

It is possible to hear a song so much that you get sick of it. Similarly, using exactly the same words repeatedly can make your audience feel manipulated and suspect your sincerity. The art of effective communication is to establish focused core themes and then to repeat them without sounding like a parrot.

Rule 6: Find a Credible Messenger

When buying a car, are you more likely to be persuaded by the salesman or by your long-time neighbor who recommends the model he owns? Most likely you will find the neighbor more persuasive. The same is true when trying to influence government. Government officials, like most of us, are influenced as much by

The Rules and Beliefs That Guide Us in the Marketing of Our Products

- Philip Morris markets its cigarettes only to adults who choose to smoke. This means that we *don't* direct our marketing or promotional efforts towards minors. We fully recognize, however, that it is often difficult to market a product in a way that is simultaneously appealing to a smoker of legal age, and unattractive to an underage smoker. This is one reason that, as a responsible marketer of a legal product intended only for adults, we *voluntarily* adhere to marketing codes.

  Click here to see information about Philip Morris U.S.A.'s marketing practices.

  Click here to see information about Philip Morris International's marketing practices.

- In addition to these voluntary efforts, there are significant legal restrictions on cigarette marketing throughout the world. Many governments have focused substantial energies and efforts on this topic.

  Click here for information about the marketing restrictions contained in the U.S. Master Settlement Agreement.

  Click here for a summary of significant international restrictions.

- We support laws mandating a minimum age for the purchase of cigarettes everywhere we do business. In addition, because many regulators and members of the public believe that *any* marketing—even the restricted marketing permitted by our codes—influences a child's decision to smoke, we make efforts to address these views and seek common ground on this issue. Our goal in every market where we do business is to stay in step with public opinion and expectations with respect to this important topic. Whether this goal is achieved through a voluntary industry agreement or through legislation, we seek a level playing field on which we can communicate to adult smokers, and fairly compete with other manufacturers.

  Click below for a few articles about the effect of cigarette marketing on smoking prevalence:

  —From the American Medical Association

  —From the U.S. Food and Drug Administration

  —Analysis of the impact of advertising bans on tobacco consumption

  Click here for references to general material about the effects of marketing on brand choice.

- Although we intend our marketing to influence brand choice by adult smokers, minors who decide to use a product—including cigarettes—appear to gravitate towards the brands that are most popular with adults. We do not accept the idea that the popularity of any of our brands among underage smokers suggests in any way that we have been marketing to minors. We think that the critical challenge is to reduce the *total* number of children who smoke *any* brand. That is what we should all focus on.

  Click here for information about Philip Morris' youth smoking prevention efforts.

  Click here for information about underage brand preferences in the United States.

Figure 7.2 Philip Morris example: Cigarette marketing practices.

those who deliver the message as by the message itself. In particular, they are more likely to be influenced by individuals they perceive as both credible and important to them—well-respected experts, for example, or constituents. A former congressman said, "I think the first thing I want to hear is: Are you a constituent or not? Are you in my state or not? Because if you're in my district and have hired people there, I'm going to pay attention to you, regardless of the merits of your case."

The observation that *source credibility* plays a powerful role in making messages more persuasive is by no means a new one. As Aristotle wrote in *Rhetoric:*

> Of the modes of persuasion furnished by the spoken word there are three kinds. The first kind depends on the personal character of the speaker; the second on putting the audience in a certain frame of mind; the third on the proof, or apparent proof, provided by the speech itself. Persuasion is achieved by the speaker's personal character when the speech is so spoken as to make us think him credible. We believe good men more fully and readily than others; this is true generally whatever the question is, and absolutely true where exact certainty is impossible and opinions are divided.[16]

Decisions about who conveys your message should not be made lightly. You have limited opportunities to access the relevant people; do not waste those opportunities by sending the wrong messenger.

Rule 7: Match the Medium to the Message

Decisions about *how* to communicate a message should not be made lightly either. You have at your disposal a variety of forums and media, including speeches, small-group meetings, newsletters, memos, interactive videoconferences, videotapes, advertising, and Web pages. News is almost always best delivered personally, in an interactive forum like a meeting at which people can ask questions. But complex technical and data-intensive arguments are usually best conveyed in written form, such as in position papers.[17]

Tailoring Framing to Specific Audiences

To meet your influence goals, you will probably need to frame your message for multiple audiences—legislators, regulators, other businesses, public interest groups, and the media, to name a few. Different audiences will find different messages persuasive.

Consider, for example, legislators and regulators. Legislators answer to constituents in their home districts and to the leaders of their parties. They are likely to respond to something that will affect local constituencies and to be influenced by members of those constituencies. Legislators are also influenced by political cycles—that is, whether or not it is an election year makes a difference.

Regulators below the top level of political appointees are relatively isolated from public opinion. They are not immune to it, but tend to focus on the technical merits of a specific proposal and on its overall impact, rather than its impact on a particular locality. According to one former government official:

> On the regulatory side, there's a different psychology involved. You have an audience to receive information, just as you do in the legislature, and they have a certain currency that they care about. In the legislatures, it's votes; it's maintaining their job, it's being able to distribute grant dollars to the home, and so on. The regulatory side is quite different. Usually people in regulatory agencies are much more mission-oriented. They have an agenda, typically, whether it's getting as many tax dollars as they possibly can for the IRS or, in environmental agencies, . . . to protect the critters and to typically move the law in that direction.

The bottom line is that framing messages for multiple audiences requires you to answer the following questions about each audience:

- What are their interests?
- What previous experiences have they had with this issue or similar issues?
- What core values could come into play?

- What uncertainties are they facing that you could take advantage of?

- Who are they likely to find persuasive (for instance, the local manager or the CEO)?

- What is the best way to communicate with this group?

Do's and Don'ts of Framing

Framing calls for you to provide plausible rationales to buttress your position without insulting the intelligence of your audience. As you begin to frame messages, consider the guidelines in Table 7.3.

Flexibility is also essential. Be prepared to change your approach to framing if what you are doing is not working. In early 2000, for example, the Clinton Administration was trying to rally support for a bill granting permanent most favored nation (MFN) trading status to China. Up to that point, China's MFN status had been subject to often contentious annual congressional reviews. Two key examples of reframing characterized this debate. First, the bill was cast as an effort to grant China "normal" trade status. The term "most favored nation" had proven to be problematic because it suggested, inaccurately, that China was getting a special deal. Second, initial efforts to drum up support for the bill had

Table 7.3   Framing Do's and Don'ts

Find out as much as possible about your audience's interests, experiences, self-images, values, and the like.	Do not misrepresent information.
	Do not use exactly the same words repeatedly.
Take advantage of biases in decision making.	Do not cram too much information into your message.
Learn or hypothesize about your opposition's arguments, and inoculate the audience against them.	Do not underestimate the opposition by disregarding potential arguments.
Find the right messenger.	Do not try to convey complex messages in sound bites.
Take into account inherent differences among your various audiences.	

been framed in economic terms: The bill would expand trade between China and the United States. This frame resonated with the business community, but it was already on board. Unions and human-rights groups strongly opposed the deal, however, and had exerted so much pressure on lawmakers that passage of the bill was in doubt. So the Clinton Administration worked to recast the debate in terms of national security: Only by enmeshing China in the world economic order would the threat of future conflict be avoided.

Anticipating Changes in the Game

You now have the basic tools you need to play the influence game. But the game itself is changing. Globalization is raising the game to new levels and altering how it gets played in existing ones. The Internet is providing a new set of tools for the influence professional. In the final chapters, we examine how these forces are shaping the future of the influence game.

PART III

LOOKING FORWARD

The forces unleashed by globalization and the Internet are transforming the influence game by altering where and how you need to play it. To stay out in front, you need to understand how the game is changing and adjust your influence strategies accordingly. The final two chapters provide guidance on how to do that.

Globalization: Can You Conduct Corporate Diplomacy?

Globalization is altering *where* the rules that impact your business get made. Issues that used to be purely the preserve of domestic government officials—such as antitrust policy and technical standards—are increasingly subject to international agreements overseen by supranational institutions. At the same time, foreign regulators (especially in developing nations) are becoming more sophisticated in the ways they deal with business. The implication is that more businesses have to be able to undertake the corporate equivalent of international diplomacy. Chapter 8 explores how you can build your capacity to conduct "corporate diplomacy."

The Internet: Are You Ready for the Level Playing Field?

The Internet is transforming the tools of the trade for influence professionals. Today, anyone with a computer has access to a wealth of information about the progress of legislative, regulatory, and judicial processes at many levels of government, and about how other players are playing the game. This information was previously available only to those who invested substantial resources. As such, it was a source of competitive advantage in the influence game. The Internet is also enabling groups whose members are widely dispersed, and thus—before the Internet—difficult to contact quickly, to mobilize to exert influence. Chapter 9 examines how the Internet is leveling the playing field and what you should do about it.

In both chapters, we make some predictions about the future of the influence game. This is a risky business: As Niels Bohr so aptly remarked, "Prediction is difficult, especially of the future." Nonetheless, we feel on solid enough ground to describe some emerging trends and explore their potential impacts.

CHAPTER 8

Globalization: The Rise of Corporate Diplomacy

Globalization does not alter the fundamental nature of the game, or the core strategies you employ to play it. You must still identify leverage points, build coalitions, and frame persuasive messages. But it does change *where* your company will play influence games. To the extent that international rule making influences you, you will have to organize to exert influence at more levels and to integrate your global government relations efforts more tightly. This chapter explores how to do that.

Playing Global Influence Games

Corporate efforts to influence foreign political processes have long been the preserve of large multinational companies and trade associations representing export industries. But issues that once were purely domestic concerns—such as antitrust policy, intellectual property protection, environmental regulation, labor standards, and so on—are rapidly becoming subject to international treaties overseen by supranational organizations such as the World Trade Organization and the United Nations. As international agreements increasingly impinge on areas that have traditionally belonged to domestic policy making, every company has to be prepared to conduct corporate diplomacy. Leading companies are finding new and creative ways to influence how government affects them at the global level.

Case Study: Negotiating Mutual Recognition Agreements

Consider, for example, the Mutual Recognition Agreements (MRAs) negotiated by the United States and the European Union (EU) and signed in 1998.[1] As we have seen, these agreements provided for mutual recognition of each other's testing organizations, allowing U.S. companies to get their products tested domestically to EU standards and vice-versa. The MRAs covered nearly $50 billion in trade in seven sectors: pharmaceuticals, medical devices, telecom, electrical safety, electromagnetic compatibility, pleasure boats, and veterinary biologics. The agreement saved U.S. and EU companies an estimated $1 billion annually in testing and certification costs.

How did the MRAs come about? Officials in the U.S. Department of Commerce initiated negotiations after a survey of U.S. executives revealed that testing products to new EC standards had become the number-one trade-related issue of concern to them. But negotiations went nowhere until a newly formed coalition of European and U.S. businesses began to push for an agreement. This organization, the Transatlantic Business Dialogue (TABD), represented the first institution created by U.S. and European companies specifically to advance trade negotiations between their governments. The TABD organized meetings of U.S. and European CEOs and government officials in Seville and Chicago that were instrumental in educating government officials and overcoming barriers to agreement.

Many of the participating companies were motivated to participate in the MRA process in order to encourage *domestic* regulatory changes. The U.S. medical-device industry, for example, was frustrated by the time it took—an average of three-plus years—to navigate the FDA approval process and bring a product to market in the United States. In Europe, similar product approvals took just six months. The industry hoped the MRA process would help to "batter down the doors of the FDA" and encourage changes in the way devices were regulated.[2] As businesses continue to seek streamlined and harmonized regulation, we can expect the power of these international coalitions of businesses to continue to grow.

Regulating the Internet

Some influence games transcend national boundaries altogether. The most prominent example is regulation of the Internet. Beyond the obvious issues of privacy and ownership of content, subtler games are being played with enormous implications for businesses. Organizations like the WTO and the United Nations are increasingly functioning as rule makers and referees in these global value-net games.

Consider, for example, ownership of domain names, the ubiquitous niftybusiness.com designations that tell users of the Internet how to gain access to companies' Web sites. The emergence of the Web triggered a new-style "land grab" in which organizations and individuals paid nominal sums to control large numbers of domain names, sometimes with the specific intent of selling them. In some cases, these cybersquatters (note the framing inherent in the term) have gained control of domain names very similar to those used by well-known corporations and either funneled away traffic or attempted to hold the companies hostage.

This phenomenon, in turn, has generated new international rule making and refereeing processes. Yahoo, AT&T, Microsoft, and Japan Tobacco sued in cases heard by the World Intellectual Property Organization (WIPO), an agency of the United Nations, seeking to gain control of domain names confusingly similar to their own corporate names.[3] In summer 2000, WIPO arbitrators found in favor of the companies, transferring control to them of domain names such as campyahoo.com, attmexico.com,

microsoftnetwork.com, and jt.com. These names had been registered by individuals and organizations located as far afield as the
United States, Israel, Austria, and Iran.

The influence of multilateral organizations on the global business environment will continue to grow. So you should think
through the implications for organization and allocation of your
company's influence resources.

Global Public Interest Games

Public interest games too are increasingly transcending national
boundaries. As these two examples of global public interest games
illustrate, these games involve public interest organizations, corporations, national governments, and supranational organizations:

1. In the late 1990s, Greenpeace launched a campaign to prevent the Stuart Shale Oil Project from developing a shale-oil
   demonstration project in Queensland, Australia. Greenpeace
   opposed the project because it would generate significant vol-
   umes of greenhouse gases. Environmental groups' efforts to
   reduce emissions of these gases are moves in a global public
   interest game that also involves governments and corporations. In this case, Greenpeace sought to pressure both the
   Australian and Queensland state governments through a coordinated e-mail and media campaign. It also targeted Suncor,
   the project's Canadian joint-venture partner. After a year's
   delay, the next stage of development was put on hold and Suncor wrote down its investment in the project.[4]

2. In July 2000, UN Secretary General Kofi Annan launched a
   "global compact" for corporations. Member companies promise to respect the environment and the human rights of their
   workers in return for recognition by the United Nations and
   the right to put a UN logo on their products. One potential
   benefit for member companies is immunization from challenges by single-issue groups.[5]

The implication is this: As the line between international and
domestic fades, you have to be prepared to influence rule making

processes that can affect your business wherever you find them. Even if you do not export anything, potential threats and opportunities can still emerge from organizations and governmental processes located far beyond your borders.

Playing Local Influence Games

Companies producing and selling internationally have always had to deal with foreign governments. But at least three developments have fundamentally altered the nature of the *local* influence games that international companies need to play.

First, the issues of greatest concern to international companies have become much more sensitive for national governments. Until the late 1980s, the focus in international trade was on lowering border barriers: tariffs and quotas. Negotiations to eliminate these barriers unfolded between national governments; companies limited themselves to building domestic coalitions to lobby their own governments. Now that such borders have been essentially eliminated, the focus has shifted to nontariff barriers, such as who gets to acquire what companies, how products get produced and distributed, who controls what intellectual property, and what standards get set for environmental protection and working conditions.

As a result, the local politics of international trade and investment have become more intense throughout the world. This is true even in the United States. In mid-2000, for example, members of Congress introduced legislation intended to block Deutsche Telecom's acquisition of VoiceStream Wireless Corporation. The legislation barred the transfer of wireless licenses to any company more than 25 percent owned by a foreign government. (Deutsche was then 58 percent owned by the German government.)[6]

Second, businesses have to deal with governments that are becoming more sophisticated in their dealings with foreign businesses. "Consistency will become a bigger issue as we see more sophistication on the part of governments in terms of looking at what their peers in other countries are doing," predicts one former trade official. "The Internet will play a big role here, because it is becoming so much easier to learn about detailed government regulations via the Internet."

With the rapid growth of emerging markets, the number of countries that companies must devote time to is increasing. In the past, even multinationals could focus most of their attention on just three markets: the United States, Europe, and Japan. Now it is no longer possible to simply overlook problems outside major markets, or to count on local government officials to roll over in order to satisfy foreign investors. The more sophisticated governments of developing countries are making decisions that will profoundly shape the business environment: Pricing, product approvals, intellectual property protection, financial systems, business and tax laws are all evolving rapidly. These are compelling reasons for companies to get involved in local political processes that will ultimately influence their success or failure in these markets.

Third, the ability of the U.S. government to have a decisive impact on foreign rule making on behalf of U.S. businesses is declining as we move toward a multipolar world economy. This is exemplified by European Community regulators' challenges to mergers of large U.S.-based companies, such as Boeing-McDonnell Douglas, WorldCom-Sprint, and AOL-Time Warner. As one senior official in the Clinton Administration observes, "Historically, to manage influence abroad, a combination of U.S. government and U.S. industry was pretty successful. And it still is, if you are talking about relatively narrow or obscure regulatory processes or legal issues. But now, particularly if you are talking about a highly politicized issue in a country, you really do have to become part of the local political process to be effective."

As a result, effective influence strategies increasingly have to combine *external influence* (for example activating the power of agencies in the U.S., EU, or supranational agencies) and *internal influence* (for example building coalitions with local businesses or other domestic interest groups) in order to have an impact on the policies of national governments. If you are trying to avoid price increases for medical devices in Japan, it is not enough to have the U.S. government on your side. You have to build coalitions with local associations, employers, and doctors in Japan.

The implication is that you will have to pay much more attention to applying the principles outlined in this book to *internal* politics within the countries in which you operate: identifying leverage points, seeking domestic allies to support their positions, and framing persuasive arguments. This is particularly true for small businesses. According to one former trade official, "Smaller companies . . . will have to work harder to develop local coalitions. Because, let's face it, small foreign companies just don't have the local clout to get things done." In seeking alliances with local joint-venture partners, for example, you should evaluate their capacity to influence local rule makers.

You also have to be prepared to exert influence simultaneously in *multiple arenas.* If you plan to grow through a series of acquisitions, for example, you may have to get regulatory approvals in dozens of jurisdictions. Acting simultaneously in multiple arenas requires very tight integration of your company's global government relations efforts. One senior administration official cites General Electric as exemplar:

> In organizing its global policy-making, GE employs government relations staff around the world. They do not use their local marketing people, because they realize that government relations work requires a different skill set, that marketing people tend not to make government relations a high priority, and that they are often not very good at it anyway. And if you think about it, you wouldn't want to put your marketing person in the position of having to tear down barriers, particularly since the people putting up the barriers are often potential customers. Using a dedicated government relations team has been a real recipe for success, and I think this is the best way to really achieve global influence.

While many companies have moved to globalize their business operations, few have truly globalized their government relations operations. Doing so requires a shift from thinking of yourself as a U.S. company (or German or Japanese or whatever) that manages political operations abroad to conceiving of yourself as a global operation that works seamlessly in local environments everywhere. Failure to make this shift can be very costly, as Bridgestone/Firestone, Time Warner, and others have discovered.

Case Study: Diplomatic Missteps at Coca-Cola

Failure to conduct effective corporate diplomacy can be very costly for companies and their leaders, as the experience of Coca-Cola CEO M. Douglas Ivester illustrates.[7]

Ivester resigned as Chairman and CEO of the Coca-Cola Company in December 1999, after barely two years on the job. A 20-year veteran at Coke, Ivester had been former CEO Roberto Goizueta's right-hand man as president of the company. He was widely admired as a tough, detail-oriented manager with a talent for making complex financial transactions work.

In part, Ivester's dramatic fall was the result of internal operational problems—a festering racial-discrimination suit, troubled relationships with Coke's bottlers—and reduced profitability due to the Asian financial crisis. But poor handing of Coke's diplomatic relations with foreign governments played a substantial role in his downfall. Ivester was apparently unprepared to manage the governmental relations that inevitably impact the local operations of global companies. "The job of running a giant company like Coca-Cola is akin to conducting an orchestra," The *Wall Street Journal* commented after his resignation. "But M. Douglas Ivester, it seems, had a tin ear."[8]

The Belgian Contamination Incident

On June 8, 1999, 33 Belgian schoolchildren became ill after drinking Coke bottled at an Antwerp facility. A number were hospitalized. A few days later, more Belgians began complaining of similar symptoms after drinking foul-smelling cans of Coke bottled at a plant in Dunkirk, France. In response, 17 million cases of Coke from five European countries were recalled and destroyed.

European officials severely criticized Coke's response to the crisis. It took the company 48 hours to explain how to identify which cans were potential risks.[9] "That a company so very expert in advertising and marketing should be so poor in communicating on this matter is astonishing," stated France's health minister.[10]

Ivester was in Paris when the crisis broke. Rather than travelling to the scene to take charge personally, he elected to fly home to Atlanta. For several days, he made no public statements. It was reported that at least one member of the board counseled him to go to Belgium and speak publicly about the incident. Ivester decided to comply with a request from the Belgian health minister to keep the matter behind closed doors and not use the press. The health minister subsequently appeared on Belgian television and criticized Coke. By acting quickly, Ivester might have gotten ahead of the curve, but his subsequent statements seemed like too little too late.

The Failed Bid for Orangina

Coke also stumbled in its dealings with French regulators over the company's efforts to acquire Orangina. In December 1997, Coke announced an $844 million deal to acquire the Orangina brand and four plants from the French beverage company Pernod Ricard. (Orangina held an 8 percent share of France's soft-drink market.) The deal was expected to boost Coke's market share in France from 49 percent to 58 percent.

Industry observers were surprised by the deal. Earlier in 1997, France's antitrust authority had fined Coke $1.8 million for anti-competitive practices in the early 1990s, following a complaint from Orangina. And Pepsi, which held a 9 percent share of the French soft-drink market, was vocal in its opposition to the deal, in part because Pernod Ricard also distributed Pepsi products in France.

After a nine-month review, the French government rejected Coke's bid, citing the extent to which Pepsi and other soft-drink companies relied on Orangina's distribution network. Coke appealed the decision and offered to allow a third party to handle on-premise distribution for a transitional period. In April 1999, France's highest judicial authority upheld the ruling.

Some saw Coke's persistence as detrimental. "It's not smart to give up all your political credits," stated one industry observer.[11] Furthermore, Coke was apparently aware early on that the French government would probably reject the deal. People close to Ivester recommended that Coke withdraw the bid before it was formally rejected. Rather than recognize that the battle was lost and shift goals, he chose to fight it out. This decision antagonized officials and did not change the outcome.

Trouble with Cadbury Schweppes

Ivester also ran into trouble when Coke tried to do an end run around EU antitrust regulators, a tactic that invariably leads to trouble. In December 1998, the company announced a $1.85 billion purchase agreement with U.K.-based Cadbury Schweppes. The agreement gave Coke non-U.S. rights to 30 brands, including Canada Dry and Dr. Pepper, in more than 120 countries excluding France, South Africa, and the United States. The deal was expected to add 2 percent to Coke's global market share.

A number of EU countries (including Germany, where Coke held 56 percent of the soft-drink market) opposed the deal, claiming that it threatened competition. Furthermore, EU antitrust authorities resented the fact that the deal was structured so that Coke could avoid seeking EU approval by approaching individual national regulators. EU Competition Commissioner Karl Van Miert insisted that Coke submit its plan for pan-European regulatory review and threatened the company with fines if it failed to comply. "They thought they could pull the wool over our eyes," Van Miert said. "They should learn to respect the rules along with everyone else."[12]

In May 1999, just weeks after revising its Orangina bid, Coke agreed to scale down its proposed purchase of Cadbury Schweppes, giving up national markets such as Germany, Italy, and Spain while retaining Britain, Greece, and Ireland. The company later ran into problems with regulators in Mexico and Canada.

A Long Hot Summer

Finally, Ivester failed to appreciate how globalization had changed the public relations game. In an October 1999 interview with *Veja*, a Brazilian magazine, he revealed that the company was testing wireless technology that would enable vending machines to change the prices of its product based on temperature. Ivester described the strategy as simply a classic supply-and-demand scenario. "Coca-Cola is a product whose utility varies from moment to moment," he explained. "In a final summer championship, when people meet in a stadium to enjoy themselves, the utility of a chilled Coca-Cola is very high. So it is fair it should be more expensive. The machine will simply make this process automatic."[13]

The interview elicited broad international exposure and critical comment. A spokesman for Pepsi seized the opportunity: "We believe machines that raise prices according to temperature exploit loyal customers and people who live in warm climates. At Pepsi, we are focused on innovations that make it easier to buy our drinks, not harder."[14] Ivester's comments angered executives at Coke's crucially important affiliate bottlers, who were the ones actually in the vending-machine business.

A few days after the interview was published, a spokesman for Coke stated that Ivester's remarks had been taken out of context. "The company is not introducing vending machines that raise the price of soft drinks in hot weather," he explained. "We are exploring innovative technology and communication systems that can actually improve product availability. We have no plans to commercialize technology that would increase pricing in hot weather. The only pricing discussions we've had . . . is how it might be able to reduce prices at off-peak times, or special promotions."[15]

Enter the Diplomat

Douglas Daft, an Australian with extensive international experience who had been president of Coke's Asian operations, replaced Ivester. Daft moved quickly to reorganize the company, transferring regional heads away from headquarters and closer to their local markets. Meanwhile, two new business units were created to manage operations throughout Europe. According to one Merrill Lynch analyst: "Daft has a wonderful manner. He makes people feel comfortable. Coke is a multinational company, operating in many different cultures. Daft is more experienced at handling these differences than anyone else in the company."[16]

Daft also immediately began working to mend key relationships, convincing a key Black executive to stay with the company, reducing the pressure on bottlers, and seeking a settlement in the racial discrimination case, which was indeed settled for $192.5

million in late 2000.[17] He also reached out to key regulators in the
United States and especially in Europe. The European edition of
the *Wall Street Journal*, for example, reported on a meeting between Daft and EU Competition Commissioner Karl Van Miert:

> Over a two-hour lunch at Comme Chez Soi, one of Brussels "finest
> restaurants," the new head of Coke and the man who had accused it
> of "trying to pull the wool" over EU regulators' eyes discussed Euro-
> pean competition law and where Coke had gone wrong. Why,
> Mr. Daft wanted to know, did Mr. Van Miert order raids on the of-
> fices of Coke and its bottlers last year? Why the continuing investi-
> gation into whether Coke and the bottlers abuse their strong market
> position to push competitors off store shelves? "I wanted to under-
> stand how he sees the situation," Mr. Daft reflected later. "The mis-
> take we made was we saw only what was legally acceptable in the
> United States. You've got to be able to look at things through their
> eyes."[18]

The bottom line is this: Ivester violated many of the basic pre-
scriptions we have outlined and he paid the price. He did not get
out in front of the contamination crisis. He allowed the company's relationships with key government officials to become
frayed, antagonizing those whose support he needed. He did not
work to sustain his own coalition with the bottlers. He underestimated the ability of opponents (e.g., Pepsi in France) to mobilize
opposing coalitions. He was insufficiently sensitive to the impact
of framing on public opinion. Finally, he did not know when to
shift his goals and so expended precious political capital unnecessarily. Daft, on the other hand, appears to understand what it
takes to run a company with global operations subject to oversight
by many governments.

Thinking Diplomatically

Ivester's problems are an example of a larger phenomenon: Skilled
senior managers who lack the ability to think diplomatically and
thus get themselves into hot water with governments. The experience of the CEO of Bridgestone, Yoichiro Kaizaki, in dealing with

the U.S. government over Bridgestone/Firestone's tire recall is another case in point. Kaizaki's skill as a hard-nosed manager in Japan did not prepare him to deal with the U.S. press or with congressional hearings into his company's actions. Rather than testify at the hearings himself or send an articulate representative, he tapped Bridgestone/Firestone's president, Masatoshi Ono, whose weak English skills and diffident manner did not play well in front of the Senate Commerce Committee. The *Wall Street Journal* reported that Ono "came across as tentative and unforthcoming in the U.S. media glare."[19]

Paradoxically, the very skills that make people like Ivester and Kaizaki so successful at running internal operations—such as strong technical problem-solving orientations and dogged determination to prevail—can become liabilities when it comes time to manage government relations, especially in crises and when dealing with foreign governments. If you find yourself in a hole, it is unwise to keep on digging.

The good news is that the capacity to think diplomatically can be learned. The training that diplomats get, principally through involvement in ongoing negotiations and rotation through foreign and domestic postings, builds their ability to:

- *Gather and use intelligence.* Diplomats quickly find out that it is tough to respond to threats if you don't see them coming. So they learn to build networks of relationships and cultivate other sources of intelligence who act as early-warning systems. Likewise, corporate diplomats need to build good intelligence-gathering systems to avoid being blindsided in dealings with foreign governments.

- *Build and maintain coalitions.* Major diplomatic initiatives, whether trade negotiations or preparations for war, invariably involve many nations. Thus their outcomes are strongly influenced by coalitional dynamics, and diplomats immerse themselves in efforts to shape and sustain shifting sets of alliances. As we have seen, companies' ability to influence foreign governments increasingly rests on their capacity to build local and international coalitions. This means, for example, getting involved with national trade associations and local Chambers of Commerce whose members are likely to have clout with both local and U.S. government officials.

- *Manage internal politics.* Internal differences can undermine a nation's ability to project influence beyond its borders. So diplomats learn to manage internal decision making in order to build the consensus necessary to conduct effective diplomacy externally. Likewise, your ability to play the international influence game well rests, in part, on your capacity to build consensus among diverse and often far-flung interest groups within your own organization. Otherwise, you risk speaking with multiple voices. In the medical-devices industry, for example, local representatives would respond to requests for information from government officials without realizing that they were undermining companywide efforts to standardize the dissemination of information.

- *Bridge disparate cultures.* By definition, the conduct of international relations involves fostering communication across cultural divides. Through foreign postings and language training, diplomats learn to act as bridges between decision makers from different cultures. If your company has to play international influence games, you need to cultivate the ability to understand differences and to organize to project influence across cultural boundaries. In part, this can be accomplished by seasoning high-potential managers with postings in foreign operations.

Use the list in Table 8.1 as a diagnostic tool with which to rate your company on each of these four dimensions. Then ask several outsiders who know your company well and will give you honest feedback to rate you on the same dimensions. If you do not possess these sorts of diplomatic skills, how will you acquire them? To what extent do your company's line executives (especially country and regional managers) need these skills? Should they get training in how to conduct corporate diplomacy?

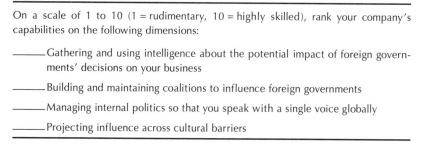

Table 8.1 Assessing Your Diplomatic IQ

On a scale of 1 to 10 (1 = rudimentary, 10 = highly skilled), rank your company's capabilities on the following dimensions:

_____Gathering and using intelligence about the potential impact of foreign governments' decisions on your business

_____Building and maintaining coalitions to influence foreign governments

_____Managing internal politics so that you speak with a single voice globally

_____Projecting influence across cultural barriers

Developing Your Diplomatic Corps

Beyond honing the diplomatic capabilities of your managers, think about whether your company needs a diplomatic corps specifically dedicated to the conduct of corporate diplomacy. If you operate globally or plan to do so, the answer is almost certainly yes. But even if you do not, it is worth thinking hard about whether you need some diplomatic expertise on staff. These days, the world can come to you as easily as you can go to it.

If you decide that you need to develop skill at corporate diplomacy, how should you go about doing so?

One fundamental decision concerns your model for organizing to influence on a global level. There are three main ways to go:

1. Devote a full-time staff, at headquarters and in the field, to the government relations function (the GE model).

2. Build a headquarters-based government relations staff with global responsibilities, and have them partner with marketing and/or sales professionals in the field to get things done.

3. Make local government relations the responsibility of in-country line managers, underlining its importance and perhaps providing some oversight from headquarters.

Your decision will flow from the assessments you made in Chapter 2 of your goals and the importance of the influence game for your business. If, like GE, you have operations that can be strongly impacted by local government actions and/or if you plan strategic moves that require tight coordination across multiple arenas, the benefits that flow from the first model are likely to outweigh the costs.

Another basic decision concerns the mix of internal people and consultants you will use to oversee your efforts. Chapter 3 addressed this question with a focus on hiring lobbyists for domestic influence games, but the same cost-benefit criteria can be applied here.

If you want to build your own diplomatic corps, how should you do so? One approach is to hire people who already have diplomatic experience. A large international insurance company hired a senior official from the U.S. State Department to help work with foreign governments. This individual's experience and connections proved invaluable in dealing with local regulatory challenges around the world. Likewise, a former British diplomat was hired by a pharmaceutical company to work on regulation and reimbursement in Europe and Asia. This accomplished diplomat was also successful in translating his experience into the business context. Given the financial rewards and the opportunity to work on interesting issues, many diplomats would find such opportunities of interest.

You can also develop people internally. Here again, diplomatic training provides a useful template: it boils down to a mix of *skills training, developmental postings,* and *action-learning opportunities.* The classroom training that diplomats receive—at the U.S. Foreign Service Institute, for example—encompasses negotiation, coalition building, media relations, cross-cultural awareness, and crisis management; these are the core skills of diplomacy.

Young diplomats then enter a cycle of roughly two-year assignments. In many ministries of foreign affairs, for example, overseas postings are alternated with assignments at headquarters so that diplomats develop local expertise but stay connected to the center and do not "go native." Often the pattern of postings (and associated language training) is explicitly designed to foster regional expertise.

Diplomats in training also get specific "action learning" assignments: short-term assignments to work with task forces or other groups on specific problems, such as a set of trade negotiations. By mixing more and less experienced people, these assignments accelerate the transfer of knowledge.

The same approaches can be used to develop corporate diplomats. A good development process would identify high-potential people and then have them undertake a rich mix of (1) familiarity with the frameworks developed in this book, (2) training in core diplomatic skills, (3) developmental postings in your company's foreign and domestic operations, and (4) action-learning assignments to accelerate knowledge transfer.

As globalization alters where the influence game gets played and the skills required to play it, the Internet is transforming the toolbox employed by influence professionals at all levels. This will be the subject of the final chapter.

CHAPTER 9

The Internet: Leveling the Playing Field

The Internet changes everything, and the influence game is no exception. Companies are building sophisticated Web sites to inform and marshal support from their employees. Public interest groups are using e-mail and Web sites to organize global influence campaigns on issues ranging from human rights to the environment to foreign investment. Politicians are acquiring powerful new tools to manage their campaigns and keep their constituents happy.

At bottom, however, the Internet is just the latest tool for doing two things that influence professionals have always sought to do: Monitor what is going on and mobilize support for their positions. What the Internet does is to fundamentally change the economics of monitoring and mobilizing in ways that are leveling the playing field. How that is occurring and the implications for your business are the subjects of this final chapter.

The Internet as a Tool for Monitoring

Information is power, and the Internet provides a great deal of information at very low cost. Not surprisingly, influence professionals have rushed to embrace the Web as a tool for staying in touch with what is going on in government. In its 1999–2000 State of Corporate Public Affairs Survey, the Public Affairs Council surveyed use of the Internet by the government relations operations of 223 companies.[1] The survey results, summarized in Table 9.1, exhibit some interesting patterns. Government relations professionals are using the Web to monitor government processes and to gather competitive intelligence, in addition to keeping track of news and the activities of interest groups.

Monitoring Government Processes

Widespread use of the Web to monitor federal and state government activity reflects, at least in part, the availability of very good Web-based services. GalleryWatch (www.GalleryWatch.com), for example, offers a leading-edge subscription service for tracking bills, getting information on committee schedules, and doing research on legislation. The company gets access to bills soon after they are filed with legislative clerks, and makes copies available immediately to its clients. Subscribers can also request notifications about significant events they need to know about. Gallery-Watch employees sit in on every committee hearing and mark-up

Table 9.1   Monitoring Percentages

Monitor/research legislative/regulatory issues at the international level	28%
Monitor/research legislative/regulatory issues at the federal level	83
Monitor/research legislative/regulatory issues at the state level	77
Monitor/research legislative/regulatory issues at the local level	24
Monitor media reports	66
Monitor/research public interest groups	45
Monitor newsgroups	44

Source: Public Affairs Council, 1999–2000 Survey, *The State of Corporate Public Affairs.*

session. They send information on amendments and voting tallies (including votes by individual legislators) to a central database. Notification software then delivers information immediately to clients in whatever form they have requested e-mail, mobile phone, fax, and so on.[2]

Other Web sites, such as www.statenet.com and www.netscan .com, offer tracking services for state legislation and regulation. Some monitoring services, such as the Library of Congress site www.thomas.loc.gov, can be accessed free of charge, though they do not provide the completeness or speed of response offered by the best subscription sites.

Gathering Competitive Intelligence

The Internet also offers rich resources for researching the activities of your competitors in the influence game. If you plan to lobby the Senate Commerce Committee about a particular bill, for example, you might want to know who has contributed to Committee members and in what amounts since the bill was introduced. You will also want to know who is lobbying for your opponents. This information can be of great value when you think about alliances, rivals, and resource planning, and it is easily available on the Web.

Suppose you wanted to find out to who had contributed to a local congressman. You could go to www.opensecrets.org, a Web site run by the Center for Responsive Politics, a nonprofit research group that tracks money in politics. Simply enter the representative's name and you get a full profile of contributions (see Chapter 5 for examples). This Web site also provides breakdowns by industry and by individual company. To track soft-money contributions, you can go to www.commoncause.org. Subscription Web sites such as the FECInfo service at www.votenet.com provide this kind of information and even more analysis.

Case Study: Analyzing Microsoft

To illustrate the power of these tools, we used the www.opensecrets .org Web site to research Microsoft's contributions and lobbying.

The first step was to get a broad overview of the computer industry's political contributions in order to see where Microsoft fits in. Summary statistics are shown in Table 9.2. In Table 9.3 we look at the biggest individual contributors and recipients. Microsoft was the industry's largest contributor in the 2000 election cycle. The company has a political action committee and also contributes soft money. In addition, individuals associated with the company make contributions directly to candidates. Let's start with the PAC.

Microsoft's PAC

Total Microsoft PAC contributions and individual contributions of at least $3,000 are shown in Table 9.4. Not surprisingly, Washington State politicians are the top-tier beneficiaries. The next tier consists largely of key congressional leaders. To focus just on House Republicans receiving high-level support from the company,

Table 9.2 Industry: Computer Equipment and Services, Election cycle: 2000 (data as of September 1, 2000)

Contributions to Federal Candidates	
Contributions from individuals	$ 8,074,335
Contributions from PACs	1,231,410
Soft-money contributions	10,874,853
Total contributed	$20,180,598
Congressional elections	
Total contributed to all candidates	$ 6,319,696
Total contributed to incumbents	3,402,163 (54%)
Total to Democratic candidates	2,814,578 (45%)
Total to Republican candidates	3,435,492 (54%)

Breakdown by chamber:

	Democrats	Republicans	Avg. Democrat	Avg. Republican
House members*	159	166	$ 5,401	$ 5,092
Senate members*	34	41	17,988	26,447

*Members for this election cycle only.

Table 9.3   Biggest Individual Contributors and Recipients

Top Contributors		Top Recipients		
Organization	Amount	Candidate	Office	Amount
Microsoft Corp.	$2,814,450	Bush, George W. (R)	President	$926,749
America Online	1,197,425	Gore, Al (D)	President	429,454
Cisco Systems	644,310	Bradley, Bill (D)	President	385,220
Oracle Corp.	641,900	McCain, John (R-AZ)	Senate	281,584
Learning Co.	571,750	Abraham, Spencer (R-MI)	Senate	182,874
Kinetics Group	352,000	Inslee, Jay R. (D-WA)	House	89,350
EDS Corp.	324,135	Clinton, Hillary (D-NY)	Senate	88,753
Gateway, Inc.	312,152	Allen, George (R-VA)	Senate	85,993
JD Edwards & Co.	301,250	Gorton, Slade (R-WA)	Senate	82,800
Loudcloud, Inc.	297,000	Robb, Charles S. (D-VA)	Senate	82,087
Digital Nation	279,000	Campbell, Tom (R-CA)	Senate	72,575
Integrated Archive Systems	271,000	Hatch, Orrin G. (R-UT)	Senate	72,305
Quark, Inc.	260,000	Giuliani, Rudolph (R-NY)	Senate	67,500
eBay, Inc.	257,750	Kerrey, Bob (D-NE)	Senate	67,088
Vertical Net, Inc.	251,000	Feinstein, Dianne (D-CA)	Senate	65,800

representatives Goodlatte, Rogan, Hyde, Chabot, and Vitter are all members of the House Judiciary Committee; Representative Hyde is the chairman. Representatives Blunt, Rogan, and Bilbray are members of the House Commerce Committee. Representative Delay wields great influence as the majority whip in the House.

This information is invaluable in assessing Microsoft's contribution strategy. Recent comments by senior executives of the company suggest that they are being much more deliberate in targeting their contributions. In early September 2000, Microsoft CEO Steve Ballmer was asked whether the Justice Department's suit against Microsoft had had an effect on the company's political contributions. "Yes," Ballmer reportedly replied. "I think we were caught unaware of the fact that our company doesn't function solely based on the technology we make. . . . We're wide-awake now, though. We've had a cold shower on this topic."[3]

Table 9.4 Microsoft Corporation PAC Contributions of at Least $3,000 to Congressional Candidates, 1999–2000 Election Cycle

| Total to Republicans: | $282,499 | | |
| Total to Democrats: | $228,500 | | |

House Candidate	Contribution	Senate Candidate	Contribution
Inslee, Jay R. (D-WA)	$15,000	Gorton, Slade (R-WA)	$10,000
Nethercutt, George (R-WA)	10,000	Murray, Patty (D-WA)	9,000
Smith, Adam (D-WA)	10,000	Ashcroft, John (R-MO)	8,000
Goodlatte, Robert W. (R-VA)	8,000	Bingaman, Jeff (D-NM)	7,500
Dooley, Cal (D-CA)	7,500	Burns, Conrad (R-MT)	7,000
Baird, Brian (D-WA)	7,000	Kyl, Jon (R-AZ)	7,000
Blunt, Roy (R-MO)	7,000	DeWine, Mike (R-OH)	6,500
Frost, Martin (D-TX)	6,000	Frist, Bill (R-TN)	6,000
Rogan, James E. (R-CA)	6,000	Snowe, Olympia J. (R-ME)	5,500
Hastings, Richard "Doc" (R-WA)	5,500	Feinstein, Dianne (D-CA)	5,000
DeLay, Tom (R-TX)	5,000	Grams, Rod (R-MN)	5,000
Dicks, Norm (D-WA)	5,000	Santorum, Rick (R-PA)	5,000
Gephardt, Richard A. (D-MO)	5,000	Abraham, Spencer (R-MI)	4,500
Dunn, Jennifer (R-WA)	4,500	Conrad, Kent (D-ND)	4,500
Eshoo, Anna G. (D-CA)	4,500	Roth, William V. Jr. (R-DE)	4,500
Bilbray, Brian P. (R-CA)	4,000	Lieberman, Joseph I. (D-CT)	4,000
Hyde, Henry J. (R-IL)	4,000	Schumer, Charles E. (D-NY)	3,500
Tauscher, Ellen (D-CA)	4,000	Ensign, John (R-NV)	3,000
Chabot, Steve (R-OH)	3,500	Lazio, Rick A. (R-NY)	3,000
Davis, Thomas M. III (R-VA)	3,500		
Dingell, John D. (D-MI)	3,500		
Gordon, Bart (D-TN)	3,500		
Vitter, David (R-LA)	3,500		
Wilson, Heather A. (R-NM)	3,500		

Soft-Money Contributions

In addition to PAC donations, Microsoft contributes soft money to both major parties. A quick search on www.opensecrets.org reveals that as of September 1, 2000, the company had donated $709,292 to the Democratic Party and $1,023,283 to the Republican Party for a total of $1,732,575 in the 1999–2000 election cycle. This is substantially more than the $774,816 in soft money that Microsoft contributed in the 1997–1998 election cycle.

As shown in Table 9.5, detailed information on the timing and destination of soft-money contributions is also available.

These data can help you figure out how the money will actually be used. Consider, for example, Microsoft's June 30 contribution to the Ashcroft Victory Committee. In 2000, Senator John Ashcroft (R-MO) was a member of the Senate Commerce and Judiciary Committees. Microsoft's contribution to his "Victory Committee" is an example of a new approach to raising and using soft money. The Republican and Democratic Senate campaign committees set up "joint fundraising accounts" for Ashcroft and his Democratic challenger Mel Carnahan, respectively. If a donor gave more than $2,000, the first $2,000 went to the candidate's campaign and the remainder to the party's Senate campaign committee. But critics asserted that there was an implicit understanding that the money would be targeted to the candidate to whose joint account it had been donated.[4] The Ashcroft Victory Committee reported raising $682,000 in the last six months of 1999.[5]

We also used the Web to search for press accounts of in-kind contributions. According to one account, the company donated $600,000 in cash and computer equipment to support the 2000 Democratic National Convention in Los Angeles and a similar amount to the 2000 Republican Convention.[6]

Individual Contributions

We also examined contributions made by individuals associated with Microsoft. A search on www.opensecrets.org turned up contributions from William Gates, Jr., and his father William Gates, Sr. (Table 9.6). Although retired, William Gates, Sr., is a general

Table 9.5 Microsoft Corporate Soft-Money Contributions
(January 1–June 30, 2000)

Date	Amount	Recipient
06/30/2000	$ 5,000	Ashcroft Victory Committee Non-Federal
06/30/2000	5,000	NRCC/Non-Federal Account
06/30/2000	50,000	DSCC/Non-Federal Corporate
06/30/2000	22,500	NRCC/Non-Federal Account
06/30/2000	20,000	NRCC/Non-Federal Account
06/28/2000	30,000	NRSC/Non-Federal
06/27/2000	100,000	RNC/Republican National State Elections Committee
06/22/2000	2,500	NRCC/Non-Federal Account
06/16/2000	25,000	RNC/Republican National State Elections Committee
06/08/2000	250	DSCC/Non-Federal Mixed
06/08/2000	250	DSCC/Non-Federal Mixed
06/07/2000	321	National Abortion Rights Action League
05/24/2000	8,985	2000 Republican H/S Dinner Trust Non-Federal
04/21/2000	453	NRSC/Non-Federal
04/21/2000	698	NRSC/Non-Federal
04/17/2000	15,000	DCCC/Non-Federal Account
04/17/2000	40,000	DSCC/Non-Federal Corporate
04/12/2000	5,000	RNC/Committee to Preserve Eisenhower Center
04/11/2000	33,690	NRSC/Non-Federal
04/11/2000	51,832	NRSC/Non-Federal
04/04/2000	30,000	2000 Republican H/S Dinner Trust Non-Federal
03/31/2000	55,000	NRSC/Non-Federal
03/30/2000	35,000	NRCC/Non-Federal Account
03/30/2000	56,542	DCCC/Non-Federal Account
03/27/2000	15,000	NRCC/Non-Federal Account
03/27/2000	25,000	NRCC/Non-Federal Account
03/07/2000	10,000	NRCC/Non-Federal Account
02/29/2000	10,000	DCCC/Non-Federal Account
02/16/2000	40,000	RNC/Republican National State Elections Committee
01/06/2000	35,000	RNC/Republican National State Elections Committee

counsel at the Seattle lobbying firm of Preston, Gates, & Ellis, which advises Microsoft on its antitrust issues; he is also associated with the Gates Foundation.

Analyzing Politicians

Not surprisingly, Senator Slade Gorton (R-WA) was a major recipient of contributions from Microsoft. Gorton is a long-time supporter of Microsoft (an article in the *Seattle Times* referred to him as "the Senator from Microsoft").[7] He played a role in the effort to reduce the budget for the antitrust division of the Justice Department in October 1999.[8] In 2000, he sat on the following Senate committees: Budget; Energy and Natural Resources; Appropriations; Commerce, Science, and Transportation; and Indian Affairs. The results of an *opensecrets* search for Gorton's top 10 contributors in the 2000 election cycle are shown in Table 9.7. The $83,950 contributed by Microsoft includes contributions from the organization's PAC, its individual members or employees or owners, and those individuals' immediate families.

Table 9.6   Individual Microsoft Contributions

Contributor	Occupation	Date	Amount	Recipient
Gates, William	Gates Foundation	06/30/2000	$1,000	Inslee, Jay R
Gates, William	Bill/Melinda Gates Foundation	06/16/2000	1,000	McCarthy, Carolyn
Gates, William	Retired	03/22/2000	1,000	McDermott, Jim
Gates, William	Preston, Gates & Ellis	02/23/2000	1,000	Baird, Brian
Gates, William	Microsoft	12/29/1999	5,000	Microsoft Corp
Gates, William		08/20/1999	250	McDermott, Jim
Gates, William	Microsoft Corporation	08/16/1999	1,000	Gorton, Slade
Gates, William	Microsoft Corporation	08/15/1999	600	Gorton, Slade
Gates, William	Retired	03/30/1999	1,000	Gorton, Slade
Gates, William		03/05/1999	500	McDermott, Jim

Source: The Center for Responsive Politics.

Table 9.7 Top Contributors to Senator Gorton's 2000 Campaign (Organization totals include subsidiaries and affiliates)

Contributor	Amount
Microsoft Corp.	$83,950
Weyerhaeuser Co.	21,786
Boeing Co.	19,700
Verizon Communications	19,250
Simpson Investment Co.	17,950
National Republican Senatorial Committee	17,500
AT&T	17,300
Northwest Airlines	15,500
Continental Savings Bank	13,350
Plum Creek Management Co.	13,000

Source: The Center for Responsive Politics.

Microsoft's Lobbying Activity

Finally, we used the *opensecrets* site to examine Microsoft's lobbying activity. The computer industry's overall expenditures for lobbying (both in-house lobbyists and consultants) were estimated to be $38,992,707 in 1998. The companies that expended the most resources are summarized in Table 9.8. Microsoft's total reported lobbying expenditures in 1998 were $3,740,000, up from $2,120,000 in 1997. Though second in its industry, Microsoft was well down in the overall rankings: The top three companies in terms of lobbying expenditures in 1998 were British American Tobacco, Philip Morris, and Bell Atlantic, each of which spent more than $20 million.

The detailed breakdown of expenditures for Microsoft shown in Table 9.9 provides more insight into how the company spent its money and who represented its interests.

Table 9.8   Computer Companies with Largest Expenditures on Lobbying

Organization	1998 Lobbying Expenditures
IBM Corp.	$5,552,000
Microsoft Corp.	3,740,000
EDS Corp.	3,310,070
Texas Instruments	2,260,000
Oracle Corp.	1,900,000
Compaq Computer	1,462,000
Sun Microsystems	1,180,000
Intel Corp.	1,100,000
America Online	1,020,000
Business Software Alliance	1,020,000
Computer Systems Policy Project	1,020,000

Table 9.9   Lobbying Firms Hired by Microsoft Corporation in 1998

Lobbying Firm	Amount Spent
Barbour, Griffith & Rogers	$600,000
Clark & Weinstock	380,000
Covington & Burling	100,000
Downey Chandler Inc.	140,000
Norquist, Grover G.	100,000
Patton Boggs LLP	20,000
Preston, Gates et al.	600,000
PricewaterhouseCoopers	80,000
Swidler & Berlin	140,000

Source: The Center for Responsive Politics from 1998 lobbying disclosure reports filed under the Lobbying Disclosure Act of 1995.

The names of individual lobbyists on the Microsoft account are also available for each of the firms listed in Table 9.9, as are the names of Microsoft's in-house lobbyists:

Microsoft In-House Lobbyists, 1998

Berejka, Marc

Bowman, Megan

Ellwanger, Kimberly

Inman, Julie

Kelly, John

Knutson, Kent F

Koenig, Eric

Krumholtz, Jack

Rubinstein, Ira

Sample, Bill

Sampson, John

Spix, George A

This information is somewhat dated, given what Microsoft went through in 1999, but nonetheless quite enlightening (see Figure 9.1). A quick search of the online archives of Dow Jones Interactive reveals, for example, that Grover Norquist, who received $100,000 from Microsoft in 1998 and $60,000 in 1997, is president of Americans for Tax Reform. (He also lobbied on behalf of the Distilled Spirits Council, the Interactive Gaming Council, and

---

Experimenting with a Search

Try doing a search for the name of one of Microsoft's in-house lobbyists on www.dogpile.com, a Web meta-search service. (It searches using 10 popular search engines.) See what you can piece together about his or her background and activities.

Figure 9.1   Experimenting with a search.

the Edison Electric Institute.) In September 1999, Norquist and representatives of Citizens for a Sound Economy and the National Taxpayers union attended three days of briefings at Microsoft's Redmond offices.[9] Two days later, the three organizations signed a letter to members of the House Appropriations Committee urging that funding for the Antitrust Division of the Department of Justice be cut. The same day, the *Washington Post* reported that Microsoft lobbyist Kerry Knott, former chief of staff to House Majority Leader Richard Armey (R-TX), met with Representative Dan Miller (R-FL) to ask him to press for the lower funding level in negotiations with the Senate.[10] Representative Miller wrote Representative Harold Rogers (R-KY), chairman of a key subcommittee of the House Appropriations Committee, that "it would be a devastating blow to the high-tech industry and to our overall economy if the federal government succeeds in its efforts to regulate this industry through litigation." Representative Miller indicated that he had not focused on the issue until Knott and Christin Tinsworth, spokeswoman for Citizens for a Sound Economy, brought it to his attention.

Adjusting to the New Transparency

We were able with minimal effort to gather a lot of information about Microsoft's pattern of contributions and lobbying activity, right down to names, dates, and places. The implications, we hope, are clear:

- Gone are the days when you could gain an edge in the influence game by investing substantial resources in staying informed about what is going on in governmental processes.

- The availability of detailed information about contributions and lobbying unquestionably enhances your ability to do competitive analysis, but the new transparency afforded by the Web is a double-edged sword. Your competitors in the influence game can do the same.

The Web has also become a tool with which rule makers, referees, and the press can learn much more about *you*. In a 1998 survey by the Holm Group, roughly 85 percent of congressional staffers reported that they accessed the Internet for news "almost daily," more than any other source of news save the *Washington Post* (which also has an excellent political Web site, www.OnPolitics.com).[11] Sites such as OneSource (www.onesource.com) are providing quite detailed information to subscribers on the operations of companies and industries worldwide.

As government officials continue to become more Web-savvy, the nature of lobbying will change. As one professional lobbyist observed, "Legislative and regulatory staff will be less dependent on the educational role of the lobbyist, because with a few short clicks they will have their own information, however good or bad that information may be."[12] The Web enables them to probe your assertions and seek alternative viewpoints.

Finally, the Web is also creating new channels of communication and coordination among governments. Rule makers in one country are increasingly able to examine rules and rule making processes in others. We expect this phenomenon to promote greater consistency in international rule making and a corresponding decline in the ability of businesses to push for different rules in different jurisdictions.

Beyond using the available tools to the best of your ability, what else can you do to deal with the new transparency? One obvious strategy is not to give away information that might disadvantage you. You should look at all company Web sites and publications with an eye to two questions: What might my competitors in the influence game be able to discern? What impressions would these materials make on rule makers and the press?

Then there is the issue of consistency. What you say in your meetings with rule makers and referees, and those who influence them, has to be consistent with what they can find out on the Web and through other sources. Otherwise you risk losing all credibility. At the same time, a well-constructed Web site can be an asset in helping to educate decision makers and other external constituencies about your company.

What the Internet Cannot Do

The Internet is a powerful tool for keeping track of what is going on, but it is no substitute for a hard-won network of personal relationships. It can tell you very little about the states of mind of participants in the political process and their networks of relationships and obligations.

The problem of figuring out what is going on in a political process is akin to the challenge facing U.S. intelligence agencies in figuring out what was going on in North Korea during the 1980s and 1990s. The United States had very sophisticated spy satellites that could provide detailed photos of every square foot of North Korea, and all the North's communications could be intercepted. But this information told analysts very little about the intentions of the North Koreans and their assessments of their situation. Electronic intelligence, while important in tracking key developments, was no substitute for (essentially nonexistent) human intelligence.

Likewise, the Internet can help you to identify *when* things change and *what* happens. But it can not give you much insight into *why* or *how* change is occurring. For this kind of human intelligence, you need relationships with people enmeshed in the turbulent flow of government processes.

The Internet as a Tool for Mobilization

Power also flows from the ability to control who communicates with whom. The Internet transforms the economics of communication in ways that fundamentally alter the influence game.

Not so long ago, communication was costly. The more people you wanted to talk to, and the further away they were, the more costly it was. People with minority opinions tended to remain isolated in small pockets, and their influence was correspondingly fragmented and diffuse. Furthermore, issues that might have mobilized people never came to their attention, and so politics remained highly local in its orientation. Finally, those who had the resources could communicate with more people across longer distances, creating competitive advantage in the influence game.

Modern telecommunications—telephone, faxes, and most recently the Internet—has made communication inexpensive, and its cost is largely independent of distance. Thus, the previously fragmented influence of dispersed groups can be aggregated in virtual communities on the Web. People from all over the globe meet in chat rooms and air their view on bulletin boards.

It is useful to think of the Internet as an *influence lens,* a tool that can gather diffuse rays of support and focus them on leverage points. The ability of virtually anyone to make use of this magnifying technology has also contributed to the leveling of the playing field.

Special Interest Groups Lead the Way

For a while, public interest groups were way out in front in the use of information technology to mobilize support for their causes. Greenpeace, for example, used its Web site to support its previously discussed campaign against the Stuart Shale Oil Demonstration Project in Australia. The Greenpeace Web site page shown in Figure 9.2 makes it easy for sympathizers to send standardized messages to key decision makers in the joint-venture companies and Australian state and federal governments.

Another interesting example is the role of the Internet in the demise of the 1998 Multilateral Agreement on Investment (MAI) negotiations.[13] The goal of the MAI negotiations, initiated by the Organization for Economic Cooperation and Development (OECD) in 1995, was to create a set of global standards to replace the patchwork of bilateral treaties governing foreign direct investment (FDI). But the MAI became a rallying point for worldwide opposition to globalization and the power of large corporations. Ultimately, the effort to undermine the talks drew a coalition of

Suncor drops shale oil over greenhouse issues

Sydney, Wednesday September 6, 2000: Today's decision by Suncor to put on hold commercial development of shale oil in Australia proves that greenhouse intensive industries are not economically viable, Greenpeace said.

Further information

See previous press releases

Read about why this press release is so important

Do something right now:

Suncor is still trying to complete Stage 1 of the Stuart Project. While the company's decision to put on hold commercial development is a step in the right direction,

Suncor must pull out of oil shale completely.

E-mail the following people and ask that Suncor pull out of oil shale development completely:

Rick George, CEO of Suncor
rgeorge@suncor.com

Peter Hopkins, Managing Director of Suncor in Australia
phopkins@suncor.com

See a sample letter

The Stuart Project is already receiving more than *A$250 million* in subsidies from the Federal and Queensland governments. It is crucially important that these governments do not give any further subsidies to the Project or to Suncor's Australian partners in the Project, Southern Pacific Petroleum and Central Pacific Minerals (SPP/CPM).

E-mail the following people and call on them to

1. withdraw existing subsidies for the Stuart Project,

2. invest existing subsidies in renewable energy and

3. no further subsidies to oil shale.

Senator Nick Minchin, the Federal Minister for Industry, Science and Resources
kieran.schneemann@isr.gov.au

Peter Beattie, Premier of Queensland
thepremier@premiers.qld.gov.au

See a sample letter

Figure 9.2 Stop press: Suncor drops shale oil project.

more than 600 nongovernmental organizations in 70 countries, including trade unions, environmental and human-rights lobbyists and groups opposed to globalization.

Many of these groups coordinated their actions through the Internet. Conspiracy theories about secret deals between big business and governments were widely promulgated and even picked up by the mainstream media. An early draft of the agreement was obtained and posted on the Web. A writer for the *Financial Times* later wrote that "network guerillas" had ambushed the talks: "The opponents' decisive weapon is the Internet. Operating from around the world via Web sites, they have condemned the proposed agreement as a secret conspiracy to ensure global domination by multinational companies, and mobilized an international movement of grass-roots resistance."[14] Over 1,000 Web sites sprang up to protest the treaty negotiations, and opponents made extensive use of e-mail distribution lists to mobilize opposition. Significantly, supporters of the talks did little to refute the often-inaccurate arguments being disseminated. The OECD and key government and industry players never organized to meet this onslaught.

We expect public interest organizations' use of the Web to organize global campaigns to continue to accelerate. As Wes Pedersen, Director of Communications and Public Relations for the Public Affairs Council, has noted, "Countering the growing influence of these cyber-powered, anti-American, anticorporate international organizations is one of the greatest challenges corporate and government affairs practitioners will face in the new millennium."[15] Early awareness of such organizing efforts, ability to get out in front of an issue, and the capacity to integrate global influence efforts will be crucial to avoid the fate of the Stuart Shale Oil Demonstration project and the MAI.

Corporate Catch-Up

Increasingly, however, sophisticated businesses are also embracing these technologies. Companies' intranet sites have progressed well beyond merely informing employees and encouraging them to get involved in government affairs. Cutting-edge sites now send e-mail-enabled calls-to-action to all employees, and in some cases to retirees and shareholders. They also facilitate communication between employees and political officials by providing preformatted letters, automatic call setups, and online talking points. Database capabilities let the company track which employees are especially active and even collect information on employees' personal relationships with elected officials.

In our interviews, telecommunications companies were repeatedly cited as representing the cutting edge in their use of these technologies, particularly Bell Atlantic (now Verizon), Bell South, and WorldCom. Our experts attributed their aggressiveness to intimate knowledge of the technologies and experience garnering grassroots support to shape the Telecommunications Act of 1996.

Politicians Take to the Web

Politicians are also embracing the Web to mobilize support for their campaigns. These efforts go far beyond tapping into supporters' personal networks to facilitate word-of-mouth (marketing via e-mail). In July 2000, for example, Voteworks.com, a privately held Internet technology company, announced a strategic alliance with the American Association of Political Consultants (AAPC).[16] Voteworks provides tools to candidates to build interactive Web sites that support voter registration, access to jurisdiction maps and voter lists, and the like. The alliance will give Voteworks clients access to AAPC online materials and AAPC consultants a new channel on which to drum up business and work with campaigns.

Databases of voter and contributor profiles are another hot product. One company, Aristotle International, has reportedly compiled a databank on 150 million registered U.S. voters, including information on their ethnicity, profession, income, party affiliation, and contribution history.[17] "Want to target for special attention just those who vote in every election?" the company's Web site asks. "'Supervoters' are designated, and you can select only those who have voted in 10 out of 10 elections, 9 out of 10, or any criteria you choose. 'Fat Cats' are registered voters who also made a contribution to a candidate sometime in the last six years:

A dollar sign pops up on the screen next to the voter's name of a 'Fat Cat.'"

Aristotle also offers campaign-management, PAC-management and postelection constituent-management software, Internet fundraising, and Internet advertising. Noting that the company had helped nine candidates for president in 2000, Aristotle's Web site states that "Our suite of e-Campaign tools help you to build an organization, influence public opinion, win campaigns, raise funds and maintain proper state and federal disclosure requirements." Figure 9.3 is a description of the company's voter- and contributor-list services and their targeting capabilities.

Back to the Future

Clearly, the Internet offers powerful new weapons of influence. As access to these technologies continues to proliferate, we expect it to contribute to a leveling of the playing field. Ambitious influence campaigns once affordable only by large organizations will become feasible for small organizations and far-flung groups of people. As one influence professional remarked, "In some ways the Internet is the great equalizer because everyone can get their message out. Corporations can always advertise their Web sites so that more people will look at them. But looking at the Internet in isolation, it is an equalizer."

This is not to say that we expect the playing field to become level. The Internet neither obviates the need for in-person lobbying nor eliminates the advantages of having more resources to invest in campaign donations and lobbying. As one government relations professional asserted, "Organizations with the funding to do heavy-duty personal lobbying will continue to be the leaders in the influence game." The Internet can be helpful, but it certainly isn't enough on its own to make an organization effective.

As you seek to use the Internet to leverage your efforts, we urge you not to lose sight of the basics. Even in the midst of this torrent of change, the basic principles and approaches outlined earlier in this book hold up very well. The Internet will streamline

U.S. Voter Lists

With Aristotle's U.S. Voter Lists on CD-ROM, Diskette, Labels or Printout you get access to the name, address and phone number of every registered voter in your district. Optional CD-ROM software gives you the power to select and sort just the registered voters you want by party, vote history, age, district, or 25 other criteria . . . Valuable information such as listed telephone numbers and income, voter history and party affiliation (where available) is appended to each voter's name for your use in polling or GOTV phone banks. We also check records against the post office's address deliverability files. Each record is compared to an ethnic surname file, and identified with an "ethnicity" code for targeted mailings to Italian, Jewish, German, Japanese, Hispanic or other ethnic groups. Additionally, each voter's record is cross-referenced against the Census Bureau's database. With information supplied by the Census Bureau, this allows you to target your mailings by income, education, presence of children, homeowner, or renter.

Contributor Lists

If fundraising is the objective, there are no superior lists of proven givers than Aristotle's Contributor Lists. Our databases consist of contributions to political candidates, parties and PAC's from individuals and corporations as reported to the Secretary of State's office.

Every name has been checked for accuracy against the state's registered voter list and against the United States Postal Service's address deliverability files. This unique process improves the accuracy of the data and allows Aristotle to provide the following additional information, which is not included with state reports:

Party Affiliation	Gender	Age
Political District	Contribution History	Telephone Number
Occupation	Employer	Postal Carrier-Route

These enhancements help reduce mailing costs, while increasing response rates, and allow your organization to target specific contributor groups. The result is cost effective fundraising.

Figure 9.3   Excerpts from www.aristotle.com.

and support monitoring and mobilizing. But you still need to build a solid foundation of goals, organization, and relationships as discussed in Part I. And developing winning strategies will still require you to do the hard work of identifying leverage points, building coalitions, and framing compelling messages as spelled out in Part II.

Concluding
Thoughts

The ways of government are complex and at times they appear mysterious. It is easy to see why many people—including more than a few of "the best and the brightest" in business—view government as alien, at once indecipherable and inherently harmful.

It has certainly not been our intent in this book to make government seem less complex than it really is; at every juncture and at every level, and especially in the Congress and the offices of the federal bureaucracy, the paths are often byzantine and the obstacles many. But while American government is indeed complex, it is not in fact mysterious. There are clear rules, clearly marked paths through the maze, and leverage points at which you can make your corporate voice heard.

And you have every right to be heard: After all, those who drafted the Constitution created a system to make the government answerable to you, not to make you subservient to the government. Here—at least in theory—the people rule.

There is a catch, though. To be heard, to have influence, you have to decide to become a wholly engaged citizen. The same government that would ideally leave us to our own pursuits also has a constitutional responsibility to look out for the interests of the nation as a whole. The deliberations of government take place amid a great din of voices representing competing interests. As much as each of us would like to be free to simply mind our own business, producing and selling whatever goods and services we can, a working democracy requires citizen participation.

Keep this in mind: Somebody will get involved, somebody will be heard, and somebody will exercise influence over government's actions. If it is not you, it may well be somebody whose interests are very different from your own.

It has been our goal in this book to show you how to play the influence game. You need to do so in order to protect your interests (defensive participation), but active involvement in governmental decision making can also be a positive act, an attempt to use the rule-making functions of government to help shape the market in the ways you believe to be best. That is why we have included examples of how a number of farsighted businesses have gained tremendous competitive advantage, both domestically and internationally, by working with, not against, government.

Merely advising you to "get involved," however, is not enough. The workings of government are so remote from the common-sense practices of the business world that even the most astute manager may simply not know how to go about the business of influencing government. Thus we have attempted, at each stage of this book, to be both descriptive and prescriptive. We have tried to show how some businesses have succeeded or failed in their attempts to influence government. We have also offered very specific advice, gathered from a host of leading practitioners, to pinpoint the strategies and organizational structures that can help you magnify your own power in Washington, at state capitals, and internationally.

As we have emphasized throughout this book, there is no one way to set up a government relations program, no one way to build coalitions, no one way to lay out a strategic plan. But there are methods that have proven successful year after year, for a wide variety of companies. We have put them before you in the hope that you too will set about the job of becoming an effective player in the government's continuing effort to shape the marketplace.

Recommended Reading

Carnegie, D. 1994. *How to Win Friends and Influence People*. 1937. Reprint, New York: Pocket Books.

Cialdini, R.B. 1984. *Influence: The Psychology of Persuasion*. New York: William Morrow.

Fairhurst, G.T., and R.A. Sarr. 1996. *The Art of Framing: Managing the Language of Leadership*. San Francisco: Jossey-Bass.

Ghemawat, P. 1999. *Strategy and the Business Landscape*. Reading, MA: Addison-Wesley.

Harries, O. 1984. "A Primer for Polemicists." *Commentary* 78, 3 (September).

Jowett, G.S., and V. O'Donnell. 1992. *Propaganda and Persuasion*. Newbury Park: Sage.

Kotter, J.P. 1985. *Power and Influence*. New York: Free Press.

Kurtz, J. 1998. *Spin Cycle: How the White House and the Media Manipulate the News*. New York: Touchstone.

Matthews, C. 1999. *Hardball: How Politics Is Played—Told by One Who Knows the Game*. New York: Touchstone.

Milburn, M.A. 1991. *Persuasion and Politics: The Social Psychology of Public Opinion*. Pacific Grove, CA: Brooks/Cole.

Nalbuff, B.J., and A.M. Brandenburger. 1996. *Co-opetition*. New York: Currency/Doubleday.

Pfeffer, J. 1992. *Managing with Power: Politics and Influence in Organizations*. Boston, MA: Harvard Business School Press.

Riker, W.H. 1986. *The Art of Political Manipulation*. New Haven: Yale University Press.

Watkins, M. "The Power to Persuade." Harvard Business School note 800–323.

Zimbardo, P., and M. Leippe. 1991. *The Psychology of Attitude Change and Social Influence*. New York: McGraw-Hill.

Notes

Introduction

1. In general, rule making encompasses legislative and regulatory action; refereeing involves regulatory and judicial action. See the detailed discussion of these processes and their nuances in Chapter 5.

2. "Fight for Internet Access Creates Unusual Alliances," *New York Times* (13 August 1999).

3. Carl Shapiro and Hal Varian, *Information Rules* (Boston: Harvard Business School Press, 1998), p. 317.

4. "Whose Info Is It Anyway?" *Business Week* (13 September 1999): 114.

5. "FTC, Toysmart Settle Online Privacy Case," *Washington Post Online* (22 July 2000).

6. "TV Manufacturers, Cable Group Agree on Digital TV Standards," *Gannett News Service* (2 March 2000).

7. "Walled Out: For Qualcomm, China Has Beckoned Twice and Then Hung Up," *Wall Street Journal* (13 July 2000).

8. "How New Tax Shelter Promised Big Savings But Finally Fell Apart," *Wall Street Journal* (21 August 2000).

9. Joel L. Klein, "The Importance of Antitrust Enforcement for the New Economy" (Speech to New York Bar Association, Antitrust Law Section 29 January 1999).

10. "U.S. to Hit Back with Heavy Tariffs against EU's Hormone Beef Ban," *Business Day* (20 July 1999).

11. "U.S.-EU Banana War Shelved for Now, But Fight Over Beef Still On," *AP Newswires* (26 April 1999).

12. "Enron: Maybe Megadeals Mean Megarisk," *BusinessWeek* (4 September 1995).

13. "More Power to India," *BusinessWeek* (22 January 1996).

14. "Disney Gives Up on Haymarket Theme Park, Vows to Seek Less Controversial Site," *Washington Post* (29 September 1994).

15. "Disney Hopes Retreat Is Better Part of Public Relations," *Wall Street Journal* (30 September 1994).

16. "Disney to Move Proposed Park to Another Site," *Wall Street Journal* (29 September 1994).

17. See note 15.

18. See note 14.

19. A survey was sent to 100 heads of government relations. Our results are based on 30 responses.

20. "Microsoft's Window of Influence: Intensive Lobbying Aims to Neutralize Antitrust efforts," *Washington Post* (7 May 1999).

Chapter 1

1. "Leading Technology Executives Form Industry Political Service Organization," *Business Wire* (8 July 1997).

2. "Disconnected: The Strategy That WorldCom Used to Become One of the World's Largest Telecom Firms Has Hit the Buffers. What Next?" *Economist* (1 July 2000).

3. "WorldCom CEO Assails Regulators on Merger," *Washington Post* (12 July 2000).

4. "Analysts Missed Call on Merger," *Washington Post* (15 July 2000).

5. "Before the Feds Nixed WorldCom/Sprint Deal, Olympia Had Doubts," *Wall Street Journal* (5 July 2000).

6. See note 2.

7. Ibid.

8. "Analysts Missed Call on Merger," *Washington Post* (15 July 2000).

9. "Big Casinos' Big Score." *Business Week* (21 June 1999).

10. "U.S. vs. Microsoft: The Overview," *New York Times* (19 May 1998).

11. The suit accused Microsoft of (1) engaging in predatory conduct by trying to drive Netscape out of business by giving away Internet Explorer, (2) taking unfair advantage of its monopoly power by tying the browser to its operating system, (3) pressuring Internet service providers (ISPs) and personal computer manufacturers into distributing Internet explorer instead of Netscape Navigator through the use of exclusionary agreements. "Strategy: History Repeats Itself," *Computing* (15 April 1999): 40.

12. B.J. Nalbuff and A.M. Brandenburger, *Co-opetition* (New York: Currency/Doubleday, 1996).

13. "Bitter Rivals Jointly Seek Major Changes in Markets," *Wall Street Journal* (1 October 1999).

14. "Dealers Thwart Factory Plans for Retail Control," *Automotive News* (30 August 1999).

15. "Tire Deaths Time Line," *Associated Press* (7 September 2000).

16. "Tobacco Industry Accused of Fraud in Lawsuit by U.S.," *New York Times* (23 September 1999).

17. "U.N. Working on World's First Anti-Smoking Treaty," *Reuters* (25 October 1999).

18. "Washington and the Web," *Fortune* (11 October 1999).

19. "DOJ Fight Hits Fever Pitch," *CNET NEWS.COM* (22 August 1996).

20. "Barnes & Noble Drops Ingram Deal Merger," *Los Angeles Times* (3 June 1999).

21. "US, Japan Reach Deal Over NTT—Pact Settles Dispute on Access Charges to Foreign Rivals," *Wall Street Journal* (19 July 2000).

22. "Rubin Decision Deals Big Blow to Winemakers," *San Francisco Chronicle* (15 May 1999).

23. "Tort Reform Law Overturned," *Columbus Dispatch* (17 August 1999).

24. A.S. Grove, *Only the Paranoid Survive: How to Exploit the Crisis Points That Challenge Every Company* (New York: Bantam Books, 1999).

25. "High-Tech Executives Seek Looser Rules on Computer Exports to China," *San Jose Mercury News* (9 June 2000).

26. "Governor Says Businesses, Republicans Joining Effort to Defeat Sizemore," *Associated Press Newswires* (26 July 2000).

Chapter 2

1. P. Ghemawat, *Games Businesses Play: Cases and Models* (Cambridge, MA: MIT Press, 1997).

2. M. Porter, *Competitive Strategy* (New York: Free Press), p. 28.

3. P. Ghemawat, *Notes on Non-market Strategy.* Harvard Business School Globalization Note Series, October 2000.

4. D.P. Baron, "Integrated Strategy: Market and Nonmarket Components," *California Management Review* 37, 2 (Winter 1995). For a more extended treatment, see D.P. Baron, *Business and Its Environment* (Englewood Cliffs, NJ: Prentice-Hall, 1996). See also P. Ghemawat, *Notes on Non-market Strategy.* Harvard Business School Globalization Note Series, October 2000.

5. See P. Ghemawat, *Commitment: The Dynamic of Strategy* (New York: Free Press, 1991); B.J. Nalbuff and A.M. Brandenburger, *Co-opetition* (New York: Currency/Doubleday, 1996); and P. Ghemawat, *Games Businesses Play: Cases and Models* (Cambridge, MA: MIT Press, 1997).

6. B.J. Nalbuff and A.M. Brandenburger. *Co-opetition* (New York: Currency/ Doubleday, 1996), pp. 67–68.

7. The term value net was coined by Nalebuff and Brandenburger in their seminal work on game theory and business strategy, *Co-opetition* (New York: Currency/Doubleday, 1996).

8. See note 6, p. 15. The concept of the value net is an extension of earlier work in business strategy, notably the work of Michael Porter on the value system. See M. Porter, *Competitive Advantage: Creating and Sustaining Superior Performance* (New York: Free Press, 1985). Porter deals with the impact of government in the context of his five forces model of business strategy in *Competitive Strategy: Techniques for Analyzing Industries and Competitors* (New York: Free Press, 1980). He also explored the impact of government on business competitiveness in *The Competitive Advantage of Nations* (New York: Free Press, 1990).

9. See note 6, p. 16.

10. For an excellent synthesis of approaches to business strategy, including the work of Porter, see P. Ghemawat, *Strategy and the Business Landscape* (Reading, MA: Addison-Wesley, 1999).

11. "Bertelsmann, Napster Agree on Service," *Wall Street Journal* (1 November 2000).

12. "Global Crossing a Political Player Wins FCC Delay in Rival's Cable, *Wall Street Journal* (23 May 1999).

13. "U.S. Pushes Japan to Open Up Public Construction Market," *Wall Street Journal* (14 January 2000).

14. "Fenced Out: U.S. Contractors Find They Rarely Get Work on Projects in Japan," *Wall Street Journal* (10 June 1993).

15 "Doubleclick Takes It on the Chin: New Privacy Lawsuit Looms, Stock Price Drops," *Washington Post* (18 February 2000).

16. "Web Firm Halts Profiling Plan: CEO Admits Mistake in Face of Probe, Privacy Complaints," *Washington Post* (3 March 2000).

17. "Regulators Endorse Self-Regulation in Privacy," *Associated Press Newswires* (28 July 2000).

18. "OSHA's Proposed Ergonomics Regulations Meet Objections from Business," *Knight-Ridder Tribune Business News* (18 April 2000).

19. "Cato Institute Study Recommends That OSHA Cease Regulating Workplace Ergonomics," *PR Newswire* (15 May 2000).

20. "Wal-Mart Store's Cutters Win Union, Lose Meat." *Wall Street Journal* (13 April 2000).

21. "Company Says It Is the Winner in East Texas Union Vote," *Associated Press Newswires* (15 May 2000).

22. "NLRB Rules against Wal-Mart; Union Vote Legal," *Dow Jones International News* (25 April 2000).

23. "NTSB Asks to Delay Crash Tests," *Detroit Free Press* (18 February 2000).

24. D. Lohse, "State Regulators Are Considering Quicker Approvals for Insurers, *Wall Street Journal* (14 March 2000).

25. See www.procompetition.org.

26. "Florida Jury in Smoking Case Awards $145 Billion in Punitive Damages," *Dow Jones Business News* (14 July 2000).

27. "FTC Clears Merger of BP Amoco and Atlantic Richfield Company," *M2 Presswire* (14 April 2000).

Chapter 3

1. The full text of the Federal Campaign Finance Law can be found at www.fec.gov/pages/fecfeca.htm. A useful guide for businesses, *The Federal Election Commission Guide for Corporations and Labor Organizations,* can be found at www.fec.gov.

2. www.commoncause.org.

3. See C. Devereaux, "Where's the Beef," unpublished case study, Harvard Business School.

4. *Time* (31 March 1997).

5. "Companies Ended Soft Donations But Still Play the Influence Game," *New York Times* (4 August 2000).

6. "Since 1907, it has been illegal for corporations to spend money in connection with federal elections. Since 1947, it has been illegal for labor unions to spend money in connection with federal elections. And since 1974, it has been illegal for an individual to contribute more than $1,000 to a federal candidate, or more than $20,000 per year to a political party, for the purpose of influencing a federal election. Soft money is money that violates these rules. It is the corporate donations, the union contributions and the large—$100,000, $250,000 or even $1 million—contributions given by wealthy individuals to the political parties. The soft-money loophole was created not by Congress but by the Federal Election Commission in an obscure administrative ruling in 1978. For years this potential loophole remained largely dormant. It emerged from this dormancy in the 1988 presidential campaign, first when the Dukakis campaign and then the Bush campaign, began aggressive soft-money fundraising. This fundraising

involved the solicitation of corporate and union treasury funds, as well as unlimited contributions from individuals." From Common Cause Web site, www.commoncause.org.

Chapter 4

1. Editorial, "Microsoft's Lobbying Abuses," *New York Times* (1 November 1999).

2. For a discussion of the power of reciprocity and other "weapons of influence" see *Influence: The Psychology of Persuasion* ed. R.B. Cialdini (New York: William Morrow, 1984).

3. See for example, D. Krackhardt and J.R. Hanson, "Informal Networks: The Company Behind the Chart," *Harvard Business Review* (July–August 1993).

4. D. Lax and J. Sebenius, "Thinking Coalitionally," in *Negotiation Analysis*, ed. P. Young (Ann Arbor, MI: University of Michigan Press, 1991).

Chapter 5

1. "Bitter Rivals Jointly Seek Major Changes in Markets," *Wall Street Journal* (1 October 1999).

2. "Seizing the Initiative on Privacy," *New York Times* (11 October 1999).

3. Information compiled from data from www.thomas.loc.gov.

4. The Constitution provides that the presiding officer in the Senate is the Vice President, who only votes in the case of a tie. The Constitution also provides for a Senate president *pro tempore,* who is elected by the full Senate to preside in the absence of the Vice President. In reality, the Vice President is rarely in the Senate and the president *pro tempore* is a ceremonial position.

5. In 1996, Congress gave the president the line-item veto—the power to approve a bill but veto portions of it—for bills dealing with appropriations, new direct spending, and tax benefits. President Clinton made use of the line-item veto on several occasions, but the Supreme Court declared it unconstitutional in 1998.

6. "The Failure of Telecom Reform," *Telecommunications* (September 1996).

7. Cornelius Kerwin, *Rulemaking: How Government Agencies Write Law and Make Policy,* 2nd ed. (Washington, DC: CQ Press, 1999), p. 3.

8. "Fiber-Optics Rivalry Goes to Court," *Washington Post* (20 July 2000).

9. "Intel May Have Violated Anti-Trust Law," *Financial Times* (14 April 1998).

10. C. Bagley, *Managers and the Legal Environment,* 3rd ed. (Cincinnati, OH: West, 1999), p. 185.

Chapter 6

1. "A Lobbying Machine Springs Up to Revive Issue of Internet Taxes," *Wall Street Journal* (29 June 2000).

2. "Airlines' Pitches for Coveted Flights Are Intense, Need Indirect Approach," *Wall Street Journal* (28 April 2000).

3. C. Devereaux, "International Trade Meets Intellectual Property," unpublished case study, Harvard Business School.

4. Lax and Sebenius (1991) proposed this distinction. See D. Lax and J. Sebenius, "Thinking coalitionally," in *Negotiation Analysis,* ed. P. Young (Ann Arbor, MI: University of Michigan Press, 1991).

5. At the time, the ASEAN countries were Brunei, Darussalam, Indonesia, Malaysia, the Philippines, Singapore, and Thailand.

6. Kurt Lewin, a pioneer in the field of group dynamics, proposed a model of social change based on the concept of driving and restraining forces. One of Lewin's fundamental insights is that human collectives—including groups, organizations, and nations—are social systems that exist in a state of tension between forces pressing for change and forces resisting change: "[The behavior of a social system is] . . . the result of a multitude of forces. Some forces support each other, some oppose each other. Some are driving forces, others restraining forces. Like the velocity of a river, the actual conduct of a group depends upon the level . . . at which these conflicting forces reach an equilibrium." K. Lewin, *Field Theory in Social Science* (New York: Harper, 1951), p. 173.

7. See M. Bazerman, A.E. Tenebrunsel, and K. Wade-Benzoni, "Negotiating with Yourself and Losing: Making Decisions with Competing Internal Preferences," *Academy of Management Review* 23 (1998): 225–241.

8. O. Harries, "A Primer for Polemicists," *Commentary* 78 (September 1984): 58.

9. IPC press release, 14 June 1988, cited in Michael Santoro, "Pfizer: Protecting Intellectual Property in a Global Marketplace," case study, Harvard Business School (1992), p. 13.

10. See note 3.

11. The idea that negotiators should gauge an agreement by comparing it to their best alternative was developed by Roger Fisher and William Ury. They coined the term "Best Alternative to a Negotiated Agreement" or BATNA. See R. Fisher, and W. Ury, *Getting to Yes: Negotiating Agreement without Giving In* (Boston: Houghton Mifflin, 1981).

12. D. Krackhardt and J.R. Hanson, "Informal Networks: The Company behind the Chart," *Harvard Business Review* (July–August 1993). See also "Authority:

Directed Deference," in *Influence: The Psychology of Persuasion,* ed. R.B. Cialdini (New York: Quill, 1993). This book is an excellent introduction to the psychology of interpersonal persuasion, exploring key processes such as a consistency and commitment.

13. In their studies of the 1940 presidential election, Lazarfeld and his associates made the early observation that people were influenced both by the information that they were exposed to and by the people who passed along the information or to whom they went for clues about "right thinking." The result was a "multistep flow" model of opinion formation. See P.F. Lazarfeld, P.L. Bereson, and H. Gaudet, *The People's Choice: How the Voter Makes Up His Mind in a Presidential Campaign* (New York: Duell, Sloan, and Pearce, 1948). See also M.A. Milburn, *Persuasion and Politics: The Social Psychology of Public Opinion* (Pacific Grove, CA: Brooks/Cole, 1991), chap. 8.

14. See "Commitment and Consistency," in *Influence: The Psychology of Persuasion,* ed. R.B. Cialdini (New York: William Morrow, 1984), p. 57.

15. David Lax and Jim Sebenius developed the concept of sequencing in the context of coalition building. See D. Lax and J. Sebenius, "Thinking Coalitionally: Party Arithmetic, Process Opportunism and Strategic Sequencing" in *Negotiation Analysis,* ed. P. Young (Ann Arbor, MI: University of Michigan Press, 1991). See also J. Sebenius, "Sequencing to Build Coalitions: With Whom Should I Talk First?" in *Wise choices: Decisions, Games, and Negotiations,* ed. R. Zeckhauser, R. Keeney, and J. Sebenius (Boston: Harvard Business School Press, 1996).

16. See note 3.

17. Founded in 1978, the International Anti-Counterfeiting Coalition had by 1997 grown to 180 members, among them trademark-based companies, law firms, trade associations, and investment firms.

18. "Oracle Hired a Detective Agency to Investigate Microsoft's Allies," *New York Times* (28 June 2000).

19. O. Harries, "A Primer for Polemicists," *Commentary* 78 (September 1984): 57.

Chapter 7

1. "A Lobbying Machine Springs Up to Revive Issue of Internet Taxes," *Wall Street Journal* (3 August 2000).

2. "General Motors Raises Stakes in Fuel Economy War with Ford," *New York Times* (3 August 2000).

3. S. Passow, "Sunk Costs: The Plan to Sink the Brent Spar(A)," Harvard Business School Case # N9-800-028, 2000.

4. R. Fisher and W. Ury, *Getting to Yes,* 2nd ed. (New York: Penguin, 1991), p. 41.

5. People tend to have a strong psychological need for consistency. For an interesting discussion, see *Influence: The Psychology of Persuasion,* ed. R.B. Cialdini (New York: William Morrow, 1984), chap. 3. See also P. Zimbardo and M. Leippe, *The Psychology of Attitude Change and Social Influence* (New York: McGraw-Hill, 1991).

6. P.N. Johnson-Laid, *Mental Models* (Cambridge, MA: Harvard University Press, 1983).

7. I. Goffman, *Frame Analysis: An Essay on the Organization of Experience* (Cambridge, MA: Harvard University Press, 1974).

8. R. Robinson, *Errors in Social Judgment: Implications for Negotiation and Conflict Resolution,* parts 1 and 2. Harvard Business School notes 897-103 and 897-104 (1997).

9. C. Devereaux, "International Trade Meets Domestic Regulation: Negotiating the U.S.-EU Mutual Recognition Agreements," unpublished case study.

10. www.sierraclub.org/cafos/news/release7-26-00.asp.

11. See for example, M. Bazerman, *Judgment in Managerial Decision Making,* 4th ed. (New York: Wiley, 1998).

12. www.philipmorris.com/tobacco_bus/tobacco_issues/index.html.

13. www.philipmorris.com/tobacco_bus/tobacco_issues/marketing_practice.html.

14. Monitoring the Future is an ongoing study of the behaviors, attitudes, and values of American secondary-school students, college students, and young adults undertaken by the University of Michigan's Institute for Social Research. Each year, roughly 50,000 eighth-, tenth-, and twelfth-grade students are surveyed. For more information, see www.monitoringthefuture .org.

15. For an accessible summary of research on communication, see "Changing Attitudes Through Persuasion," chap. 4 in *The Psychology of Attitude Change and Social Influence* ed. P.G. Zimbardo and M.R. Lieppe (New York: McGraw-Hill, 1991).

16. Aristotle, *Rhetoric,* vol. 2, bk. 1, chap. 2, *The Complete Works of Aristotle,* ed. Jonathan Barnes (Princeton: Princeton University Press, 1984).

17. See note 15.

Chapter 8

1. C. Devereaux, "Negotiating the U.S.-EU Mutual Recognition Agreements," unpublished case study, Harvard Business School (2000).

2. See note 1.

3. "U.N. Rules for Yahoo!, Others in Disputes over Domain Names," *The Associated Press* (1 August 2000).

4. "Suncor Plans to Resolve Operating Issues at Oil Shale Project, Decides to Write Down Asset and Put Next Stage of Development on Hold" (5 September 2000). www.suncor.com/newsrelease/FinanceandStock /FinanceandStock-Other/8-334.html.

5. See www.unglobalcompact.org.

6. "Deutsche Telecom to Pay $50 Billion for U.S. Company," *New York Times* (24 July 2000).

7. This section draws on C. Reavis, "The Coca-Cola Company (A): The Rise and Fall of M. Douglas Ivester." Case study 800-355, Harvard Business School.

8. "Clumsy Handling of Many Problems Cost Ivester Coca-Cola Board's Favor," *Wall Street Journal* (17 December 1999).

9. "Can Douglas Ivester End Coke's Crisis?" *Wall Street Journal* (18 June 1999).

10. "Massive Recall: How Coca-Cola's Controls Fizzled Out around Europe," *Asian Wall Street Journal* (30 June 1999).

11. "Clumsy Handling of Many Problems . . ." *Wall Street Journal* (17 December 1999).

12. "Crunch Time for Coke," *Fortune* (19 July 1999).

13. "The Real Sting! Could Price of a Coke Rise on Hotter Days?" *Daily Mail* (29 October 1999).

14. See note 13.

15. See note 13.

16. Garth Alexander, "Coke Takes an Axe to Its Big Bad Wolf," *News International* (12 December 1999).

17. Coke Settles Bias Suit for $192.5 Million—Outside Panel Will Monitor Company's Activities," *Wall Street Journal* (17 November 2000).

18. "New Coke Chief Tries to See through Eyes of the World—Daft Mends Fences, Gains Insight in Europe," *Wall Street Journal Europe* (23 June 2000).

19. "Bridgestone Boss Has Toughness, But Is That What Crisis Demands?" *Wall Street Journal* (12 September 2000).

Chapter 9

1. Public Affairs Council, 1999–2000 Survey, *The State of Corporate Public Affairs*.

2. "A Lobbyist's Best Friend," *Forbes* (29 August 2000).

3. "Ballmer Acknowledges Antitrust Case Has Affected Political Contributions," *Associated Press Newswires* (12 September 2000).

4. "Carnahan, Ashcroft Use Loophole, Reap $1 million in 'Soft' Money, Critics Say Practice Evades Intent of Statute," *St. Louis Post-Dispatch* (24 February 2000).

5. See note 4.

6. See note 3.

7. "The Lion in Summer—The Long Road of Slade Gorton," *Seattle Times* (11 July 1999).

8. "Microsoft Targets Funding for Antitrust Office," *Washington Post* (15 October 1999).

9. See note 8.

10. See note 8.

11. *Opinion Leader Survey,* The Holm Group, October 1998 cited in *Public Affairs Review,* 2000 Annual Report of the Public Affairs Council.

12. M. Kraus, "Welcome to the World of 'Glocal' Public Affairs," *Public Affairs Review,* 2000 Annual Report of the Public Affairs Council.

13. C. Devereaux, "A Virtual Defeat? Stalling the Multilateral Agreement on Investment," unpublished case study, Harvard Business School.

14. Guy de Jonquieres, "Network Guerrillas," *Financial Times* (29 April 1998).

15. Quoted in M. Kraus, see note 12.

16. "Voteworks.com Teams with the American Association of Political Consultants," *M2 Presswire* (12 July 2000).

17. "Voter Profiles Are Selling Briskly as Privacy Issues Are Raised," *New York Times* (9 September 2000).

Index